Drunk Driving

OTHER BOOKS OF RELATED INTEREST

Drunk Driving

Louise I. Gerdes, *Book Editor*

David L. Bender, *Publisher*
Bruno Leone, *Executive Editor*
Bonnie Szumski, *Editorial Director*
Stuart B. Miller, *Managing Editor*
Brenda Stalcup, *Series Editor*

Contemporary Issues
Companion

Greenhaven Press, Inc., San Diego, CA

Every effort has been made to trace the owners of copyrighted material. The articles in this volume may have been edited for content, length, and/or reading level. The titles have been changed to enhance the editorial purpose. Those interested in locating the original source will find the complete citation on the first page of each article.

Library of Congress Cataloging-in-Publication Data

Drunk driving / Louise I. Gerdes, book editor.
    p.   cm. — (Contemporary issues companion)
    Includes bibliographical references and index.
    ISBN 0-7377-0459-4 (pbk. : alk. paper). —
ISBN 0-7377-0460-8 (lib. : alk. paper)
    1. Drunk driving. I. Gerdes, Louise I. II. Series.

HE5620.D7 D7793 2001
363.12'514—dc21
                                          00-037139
                                            CIP

©2001 by Greenhaven Press, Inc.
P.O. Box 289009, San Diego, CA 92198-9009

Printed in the U.S.A.

CONTENTS

Chapter 4: Legal Issues Concerning Drunk Driving

FOREWORD

In the news, on the streets, and in neighborhoods, individuals are confronted with a variety of social problems. Such problems may affect people directly: A young woman may struggle with depression, suspect a friend of having bulimia, or watch a loved one battle cancer. And even the issues that do not directly affect her private life—such as religious cults, domestic violence, or legalized gambling—still impact the larger society in which she lives. Discovering and analyzing the complexities of issues that encompass communal and societal realms as well as the world of personal experience is a valuable educational goal in the modern world.

Effectively addressing social problems requires familiarity with a constantly changing stream of data. Becoming well informed about today's controversies is an intricate process that often involves reading myriad primary and secondary sources, analyzing political debates, weighing various experts' opinions—even listening to firsthand accounts of those directly affected by the issue. For students and general observers, this can be a daunting task because of the sheer volume of information available in books, periodicals, on the evening news, and on the Internet. Researching the consequences of legalized gambling, for example, might entail sifting through congressional testimony on gambling's societal effects, examining private studies on Indian gaming, perusing numerous websites devoted to Internet betting, and reading essays written by lottery winners as well as interviews with recovering compulsive gamblers. Obtaining valuable information can be time-consuming—since it often requires researchers to pore over numerous documents and commentaries before discovering a source relevant to their particular investigation.

Greenhaven's Contemporary Issues Companion series seeks to assist this process of research by providing readers with useful and pertinent information about today's complex issues. Each volume in this anthology series focuses on a topic of current interest, presenting informative and thought-provoking selections written from a wide variety of viewpoints. The readings selected by the editors include such diverse sources as personal accounts and case studies, pertinent factual and statistical articles, and relevant commentaries and overviews. This diversity of sources and views, found in every Contemporary Issues Companion, offers readers a broad perspective in one convenient volume.

In addition, each title in the Contemporary Issues Companion series is designed especially for young adults. The selections included in every volume are chosen for their accessibility and are expertly edited in consideration of both the reading and comprehension levels

7

of the audience. The structure of the anthologies also enhances accessibility. An introductory essay places each issue in context and provides helpful facts such as historical background or current statistics and legislation that pertain to the topic. The chapters that follow organize the material and focus on specific aspects of the book's topic. Every essay is introduced by a brief summary of its main points and biographical information about the author. These summaries aid in comprehension and can also serve to direct readers to material of immediate interest and need. Finally, a comprehensive index allows readers to efficiently scan and locate content.

The Contemporary Issues Companion series is an ideal launching point for research on a particular topic. Each anthology in the series is composed of readings taken from an extensive gamut of resources, including periodicals, newspapers, books, government documents, the publications of private and public organizations, and Internet websites. In these volumes, readers will find factual support suitable for use in reports, debates, speeches, and research papers. The anthologies also facilitate further research, featuring a book and periodical bibliography and a list of organizations to contact for additional information.

A perfect resource for both students and the general reader, Greenhaven's Contemporary Issues Companion series is sure to be a valued source of current, readable information on social problems that interest young adults. It is the editors' hope that readers will find the Contemporary Issues Companion series useful as a starting point to formulate their own opinions about and answers to the complex issues of the present day.

INTRODUCTION

It was springtime in Fair Oaks, California, and thirteen-year-old Cari Lightner was walking with a friend along a quiet suburban street on her way to a church carnival. Clarence William Busch was driving down the same street that day in May 1980; he had been drinking, and although it was broad daylight, he struck Cari. The force of the impact threw her more than 120 feet, killing her instantly. Busch fled the scene: He had already been arrested for drunk driving four times previously, and his last arrest had been only two days earlier. When Busch was arrested shortly after the accident, his blood alcohol concentration was .20 percent.

Later in the year, Cari's mother encountered two highway patrolmen taking measurements on the road where her daughter had been killed. Candy Lightner stopped and asked the officers if Busch would be sent to prison for killing her daughter. Based on their prior experience with similar cases, they advised Lightner that there was little chance that Busch would serve any time at all. That, according to the patrolmen, was the way the system worked. Lightner was furious, but she felt helpless against the legal system.

Before 1980, fatalities caused by drunk drivers were considered tragedies, but few blamed the driver. In most states, drunk driving was treated much like any other traffic violation. Because those who caused fatal accidents while driving under the influence of alcohol did not intend to kill their victims, they often received only a verbal reprimand, a fine, or probation for vehicular manslaughter. In 1971, for example, drunk driving was not a crime in Tennessee, so when a seventeen-year-old drunk driver collided with a car that exploded on impact—killing two children and severely burning both parents—the driver received only two months' probation for vehicular homicide. Even in California, a state known for safety legislation, the laws concerning motor fatalities did not punish drunk drivers more harshly than reckless drivers. In Busch's case, he plea-bargained to vehicular manslaughter and received a two-year sentence, which he served at a work camp and in a halfway house.

The attitudes of businesses that sold and served alcohol were also much different before the 1980s. Although some states had dram shop laws that held commercial vendors of alcohol liable for any damage caused by drunk patrons, the lawyers who represented these businesses interpreted the laws in a way that would shield sellers from liability rather than provide victims with compensation. Rarely were businesses held accountable for the damage caused by drunk patrons whose decision to drive resulted in injury or death.

Cultural attitudes toward drinking were more tolerant in the 1960s and 1970s. Having cocktails during a business lunch was an accepted aspect of professional life, and overindulgence in alcohol at parties and nightclubs was part of social life. People laughed at Dean Martin as he slurred his words and staggered across the television screen with a cocktail in hand. Other TV programs and motion pictures portrayed drinking as a natural accompaniment to romance and celebration. Drinking was sophisticated; for many teenagers it marked the transition into maturity.

Of course, people who drank socially often had to travel the roadways. However, few of those who drank and drove thought of themselves as engaging in criminal behavior. According to Dwight B. Heath, an anthropologist at Brown University who studies behavior related to alcohol, "There was a time when drunk driving was treated pretty much as a joke, like some kid caught with his hand in the cookie jar." An arrest for driving under the influence was simply an inconvenience or an embarrassment. It had little impact on the driver's life—perhaps a black mark on his or her driving record that would be removed in time.

But drunk driving was no joke to those who had been injured by a drunk driver or to the surviving family members of someone who had been killed in a drunk driving accident. For these people, fatalities caused by drunk drivers were not simply unfortunate accidents but tragedies that could have been avoided; they were irresponsible—even criminal—acts perpetrated by individuals who chose to drive while impaired. If someone decided to drive while inebriated and then caused an accident, these victims felt, that person should be harshly punished and prevented from repeating the act. The existing laws offered little justice for the victims, however, and many became angry over this state of affairs. Candy Lightner points out that "people whose loved one died as the result of a crime [typically were] very angry, not only at the killers, but at the criminal justice system." Her anger over Busch's mild punishment for the death of her daughter led Lightner to start an organization to raise public awareness about the problem of drunk driving. Since anger and frustration unified the early members, it seemed appropriate to call the organization MADD, for Mothers Against Drunk Drivers.

Over the years, MADD evolved from a one-woman crusade to an organization with more than 3 million members nationwide. From the initial chapter begun by Lightner in August 1980, MADD quickly grew to 92 chapters in October 1982, and to 340 by April 1985. By the early 1980s, a full-blown social movement had begun to emerge that stirred public outrage, garnered media attention, and prompted important legal and cultural changes regarding drunk driving. MADD was joined in these efforts by a number of other early organizations, including Remove Intoxicated Drivers (RID), Boost Alcohol Consciousness Concerning the Health of University Students (BACCHUS), Alliance Against

Intoxicated Motorists (AAIM), and Students Against Drunk Driving (SADD). However, MADD remained by far the largest, the best financed, and the most well known to the public of all these organizations. Since MADD's inception, public awareness about the problem of drunk driving has improved dramatically, and attitudes toward drinking and driving have changed significantly.

With the support of law enforcement and traffic safety organizations, MADD began a nationwide public education campaign that popularized the slogan "Friends don't let friends drive drunk." MADD aired celebrity TV spots, put up billboards, and distributed bumper stickers promoting the slogan, which became so common that most people in the United States and Canada could immediately recognize it. The campaign brought the tragedy of drunk driving closer to home, hoping to inspire people to take responsibility for not only their own decisions but also the actions of their loved ones.

Another public information effort was the red ribbon project, established in 1986, in which MADD distributed 1 million red ribbons to motorists who pledged to drive safely and soberly during the Christmas and New Year holidays. In addition, MADD and its supporters began the "designated driver" campaign, encouraging merry-makers to designate one individual who would remain sober during social gatherings that involved alcohol in order to drive everyone home safely. Businesses and communities became involved, instituting such innovations as arranging for taxicab companies and transit systems to offer free rides to drinking revelers on holidays such as New Year's Eve.

Besides these and other public education campaigns, MADD also lobbied vigorously for legislative changes. As a result, in the 1980s and early 1990s, new laws were enacted that were designed to help deter drunk driving and to punish those who drove drunk. By 1996, most states had adopted laws making it a criminal offense to drive with a blood alcohol concentration (BAC) above the legal limit, which is usually .10 or .08 percent. Under these laws, drivers can be convicted of drunk driving if their BAC level is above the legal limit, even if they have not broken any other traffic laws.

One of MADD's earliest and most successful lobbying efforts focused on the tragedy of teen drunk driving. Prior to the mid-1980s, the minimum drinking age from state to state varied between eighteen to twenty-one. Because young people between the ages of fifteen and twenty make up the largest percentage of alcohol-related fatalities, MADD lobbied for laws that would raise the minimum legal drinking age to twenty-one. In 1984, President Ronald Reagan signed into law a bill requiring that the states enact such legislation, and by 1988, all fifty states had done so. In a statement made in 1997, Advocates for Highway and Auto Safety and MADD reported that "since 1985, the nationwide 21 drinking age law is credited with saving more than 10,000 lives of Americans between the ages of 15 to 20." Research has shown that raising the minimum legal drinking age to twenty-one resulted in a 10 to 15 percent decline in alcohol-related traffic deaths among teenagers. To further reduce drunk driving fatalities among teenagers, President Bill Clinton signed legislation in 1995 that encouraged the states to enact zero-tolerance laws, which would make it illegal for individuals under twenty-one to drive after having drunk any alcohol at all. By 1998, all the states had complied by passing such laws.

Public pressure by grassroots organizations also compelled the states to address another specific offender: the habitual drunk driver. Research has revealed that a disproportionate number of drunk driving accidents are caused by repeat offenders, who continue to drive while inebriated despite many arrests. The states have implemented a variety of measures to keep these repeat offenders off the road. Some states have passed laws requiring the confiscation, suspension, or revocation of the licenses of individuals who have been previously convicted of drunk driving. Other states have enacted laws that require repeat offenders to receive treatment and supervised rehabilitation or to serve jail time in detention facilities specifically designed for drunk driving offenders. Another approach is to physically prevent repeat offenders from driving, by either impounding their motor vehicles or installing ignition interlock devices that keep the vehicle from starting if the driver is inebriated.

The enactment of such legislation, combined with increased public awareness, had led to noticeable improvements by 1996. For example, the estimated number of alcohol-related traffic fatalities in the United States had dropped 32 percent from 1982. Only 40.9 percent of highway fatalities were estimated to be alcohol-related, down from 57.3 percent in 1982. Of these alcohol-related fatalities, 32 percent occurred in crashes involving a BAC of 0.10 or higher, down from 46.3 percent in 1982. Such statistics demonstrated that in many respects, the campaign to reduce alcohol-related traffic accidents was having a positive impact.

However, the 1996 statistics also revealed a disconcerting fact: Drunk driving fatalities were on the rise. Some commentators suspected that the successes had led to complacency about the problem of drunk driving. They argued that the general public had come to believe the drunk driving problem was solved and had therefore ceased to be concerned with preventive measures, leading to a new increase in fatalities. As Katherine Prescott, national president of MADD, stated in 1997, "[The public has] heard so much about drunk driving that there is a perception that it's a problem either fixed or almost fixed."

Another contributing factor appears to be the lenient attitude toward drunk driving that exists in certain jurisdictions. The states with the worst record for alcohol-related traffic deaths in 1998—Montana, Wyoming, New Mexico, and Nevada—have been continually resistant to attempts at cracking down on drunk driving. These sparsely populated states are imbued with a century-old cowboy culture of rugged individualism and self-reliance that often fosters a hard-drinking lifestyle. According to Toni Reichenbach, state director of victim services for the Wyoming chapter of MADD: "This is a good ol' boy state. You measure the distance from one town to another by the number of six packs it takes you to drink." Although alcohol-related traffic fatalities have fallen in New Mexico since the state lowered the BAC level to .08, lawmakers in states like Wyoming remain divided over passing similar legislation. They are reluctant to enact any laws that would limit the rights of individuals, even if the laws are designed to save lives.

Other commentators believe that the recent rise in drunk driving fatalities is largely due to a group of hardcore drunk drivers who have proven to be especially resistant to measures designed to reduce drunk driving. Prescott maintains, "The problem may be down to a hard core of alcoholics who do not respond to public appeals." Neither do these individuals appear to respond to stricter penalties for drunk driving: Most of the research on hardcore drunk drivers in Canada, the United States, and Europe has found that even when communities institute harsh sanctions for repeat offenders, they do not experience significant long-term reduction in drunk driving fatalities. No matter how many preventive steps communities take toward curbing hardcore drunk drivers, including the threat of long prison sentences, most remain undeterred. For instance, Busch claimed that he would never drink again, but in April 1984 he was arrested for drunk driving after hitting another victim not far from where he killed Cari Lightner. In October 1992, Busch was again convicted for drunk driving, but this time in Wisconsin and as a first-time offender because his record had been clean for five years. Many researchers agree that no sanctions are truly effective for those made impervious to punishment by long-term abuse of alcohol and by the antisocial behavior that accompanies it.

Since punishment seems ineffective as a deterrent, some social scientists recommend long-term treatment programs for hardcore drunk drivers. Recent studies show a significant reduction in alcohol-related fatalities for those hardcore drunk drivers involved in such treatment. However, an impaired driver must be caught before the court can order treatment, which limits the effectiveness and scope of these programs.

Prevention programs, tougher deterrence, wider enforcement, longer suspensions, mandatory treatment—all of these measures prevent some drunk driving tragedies, but even combined, they have not yet eliminated the problem. As the controversy continues over the best solution, the following facts remain: Drunk driving is the most frequently committed violent crime in America, and alcohol-related crashes are the leading cause of death for people aged five to fifty-four. In the words of President Clinton, "There is hardly a family or community in America that hasn't been touched by drunk driving."

Attitudes toward drinking and driving have varied over the years from acceptance to outrage, but just how far the state and federal government should go to protect citizens remains the subject of debate. To illuminate these issues, the authors in *Drunk Driving: Contemporary Issues Companion* examine the nature and scope of the problem of drunk driving as well as possible solutions. Drunk driving will continue to remain an important issue of concern, for as a MADD spokesperson states, "One life lost to a drunken driver is one too many."

CHAPTER 1

THE PROBLEM OF DRUNK DRIVING

THE SCOPE OF THE DRUNK DRIVING PROBLEM

Margaret C. Jasper

As a result of increased public awareness and more stringent leg-islation, drunk driving fatalities have decreased in the United States since 1966. Despite this improvement, Margaret C. Jasper contends, many people are still injured or killed every year as a result of drunk driving. In the following excerpt from her book *Drunk Driving Law*, Jasper summarizes the statistics on drunk driving, including the number of arrests and the various factors that influence drunk driving behavior. In addition, she reviews some of the state laws designed to reduce drunk driving. Jasper is an attorney, author, and editor who practices law in South Salem, New York.

According to the National Highway Traffic Safety Administration (NHTSA), almost 1.4 million people have died in traffic crashes in the United States since 1966. During the late 1960's and early 1970's, more than 50,000 people lost their lives each year on the nation's public roads and highways, and more than half of the drivers killed had been drinking.

Because traffic safety has improved since that time, in large part due to legislation which created the NHTSA in 1966, the annual death rate has declined considerably, to about 40,000, even though the number of drivers, vehicles and miles driven have all greatly increased. As reported by the NHTSA, the fatality rate per 100 million vehicle miles traveled fell from 5.5 in 1966 to 1.7 in 1996, which is a 69 percent improvement over three decades. Using miles traveled as a measuring stick, the likelihood of being killed in a traffic accident in 1966 was more than three times what it is today.

Alcohol-Related Traffic Accidents

Nevertheless, despite these dramatic improvements in traffic safety, an average of more than 115 people still die each day from motor vehicle accidents in the United States, and it is estimated that 41 per-cent of the drivers who die in crashes have been drinking.

Excerpted from Margaret Jasper, *Drunk Driving Law*, a volume in the Law for the Layperson Legal Almanac Series, published in 1999 by Oceana Publications, Inc., Dobbs Ferry, NY; www.oceanalaw.com. Reprinted with permission.

Drinking and driving is the most frequently committed violent crime in America. Since 1989, four times as many Americans died in drunk driving crashes as were killed in the Vietnam War. Between 1982 and 1995, approximately 300,274 persons lost their lives in alcohol-related traffic crashes.

According to the NHTSA, somebody dies in an alcohol-related crash every thirty minutes. It is estimated that about two in every five Americans will be involved in an alcohol-related crash at some time in their lives. The NHTSA also estimates that one out of every 280 babies born today will die in an automobile accident with an intoxicated driver. In fact, traffic crashes are the major cause of death for children age 0–14, and 21.4 percent of those deaths are alcohol-related.

Drinking and driving-related injuries and fatalities have become so prevalent that concerted efforts to combat the problem have increased during the 1990's. Many organizations have emerged to increase public awareness and have successfully lobbied for the passage and enforcement of more stringent drunk driving laws. In fact, according to the NHTSA, more than 2,300 anti-drunk driving laws have been passed since 1980.

As a result of these efforts, there has been a significant decrease in alcohol-related traffic fatalities since 1989. According to the NHTSA, in 1986, there were 24,050 alcohol-related fatalities compared to 16,189 in 1997—a 32 percent decrease. Nevertheless, despite efforts to deter drunk driving, alcohol-related traffic fatalities still pose a grave and dangerous problem.

In 1997, 16,189 people were killed in alcohol-related accidents. These deaths constituted approximately 38.6 percent of the total 41,967 traffic fatalities for the year. In addition to the fatalities, approximately 1,058,990 people were injured in alcohol-related accidents—an average of one person injured every 30 seconds. Due to these accidents, approximately 30,000 people a year suffer permanent work-related disabilities.

Alcohol impairment is a known contributor to motor vehicle accidents. It is a misconception, however, that one must be "drunk" in order to be a dangerous driver. Many alcohol-impaired drivers do not appear visibly drunk. Studies have indicated that even small amounts of alcohol can impair driving skills.

Another common misbelief is that the likelihood of impairment is contingent on the type of drink. Some mistakenly believe that beer, for instance, is less likely to cause impairment compared to hard liquor. However, impairment is not determined by the type of drink. It is measured by the amount of alcohol ingested over a specific period of time. In fact, beer is the most common drink consumed by people stopped for alcohol-impaired driving or involved in alcohol-related crashes.

Many believe that they have had enough time to "sober up"

between the time they drink and the time they drive, and are unaware of how much time is actually needed for one's body to metabolize alcohol. Studies indicate that most people need at least one hour to metabolize one drink. . . .

The Costs of Drunk Driving

According to the NHTSA, automobile crashes claim about 42,000 lives each year in the United States. The associated costs to society are overwhelming: economic costs ($150 billion including $19 billion in medical care and emergency expenses); lost productivity ($42 billion); property damage ($52 billion); and miscellaneous crash-related costs ($37 billion). Approximately 30 percent of these automobile accidents are alcohol-related, accounting for $45 billion in associated costs each year. This figure does not include pain, suffering and lost quality of life, which significantly raise that figure.

The cost for each injured survivor of an alcohol-related crash averaged $67,000, including $6,000 in health care costs and $13,000 in lost productivity. In addition, over 25 percent of the first year of medical costs for persons hospitalized as a result of an automobile crash are paid by tax dollars, about two-thirds through Medicaid and one-third through Medicare.

Examining Drunk Driving Accidents

Accidents involving men are much more likely to be alcohol-related than those involving women. Among fatally injured male drivers of passenger vehicles in 1997, 37 percent had blood alcohol concentrations (BACs) of 0.10 percent or more and were age 31–40. The corresponding proportion among women was 17 percent, the majority of which fell in the same age group.

Since 1980, the proportion of fatally injured passenger vehicle drivers with BACs at or above 0.10 percent declined more among drivers 16–20 years of age than among older drivers.

Alcohol-related accidents may occur at any time of day; however, the incidence peaks at night and increases on weekends and holidays. According to the Insurance Institute for Highway Safety (IIHS), in 1997, 66 percent of passenger vehicle drivers with BACs at or above 0.10 percent were fatally injured between midnight and 3 AM, compared with 7 percent between 9 AM and noon.

In addition, forty-three percent of all drivers fatally injured on the weekends—defined as 6 PM Friday to 6 AM Monday—had BACs of 0.10 percent or more. During the rest of the week, the proportion was 23 percent.

According to the NHTSA, in single-vehicle crashes occurring on weekend nights in 1994, 72.3 percent of the fatally injured drivers 25 years of age or older were intoxicated, as compared with 57.7 percent of drivers under the age of 25.

Holiday periods also account for a disproportionate number of alcohol-related traffic accidents. As may be expected, of all the accidents which occurred on New Years Eve/Day in 1997, the largest percentage were alcohol-related (67 percent).

According to IIHS statistics, since 1980, the percentage of fatally injured people with BACs at or above 0.10 percent has declined among passenger vehicle drivers, tractor-trailer drivers and motorcyclists. In 1981, the proportion of passenger vehicle driver deaths involving BACs at or above 0.10 percent was 54 percent, compared with 31 percent for 1997, and the proportion of motorcyclist deaths involving BACs at or above 0.10 percent was 46 percent in 1980, compared with 34 percent in 1997.

The group of drivers with the greatest decline in alcohol-related fatalities is tractor-trailer drivers. In 1980, the proportion of fatally injured tractor-trailer drivers with BACs at or above 0.10 percent was 15 percent, compared with 3 percent in 1997.

Many states are lowering their BAC to define impaired driving from 0.10 percent to 0.08 percent, based on studies demonstrating the sharp decline in driving ability above this level.

According to the IIHS, the probability of an automobile crash begins to significantly increase at 0.05 percent BAC and climbs rapidly after 0.08 percent BAC. Among drivers with BACs above 0.15 percent, the likelihood of dying in a single-vehicle crash during weekend nights is more than 380 times higher than for drivers who do not drink.

Many states have also enacted "zero tolerance" laws which set the BAC for young drivers even lower—0.00 to 0.02 percent—in large part based on studies showing a BAC as low as 0.02 percent negatively impacts driving ability. Zero tolerance laws have been found to reduce the incidence of alcohol-related automobile crashes involving young drivers by 20 percent.

Drunk Driving

According to the FBI, arrests for driving while under the influence (DUI) and driving while impaired (DWI) resulted in one of the highest arrest counts categorized in 1994—at 1.4 million—the same number of arrests for drug abuse violations and slightly higher than arrests for larcenies (1.5 million). In addition, of the 14.6 million arrests for criminal infractions in 1994, driving under the influence was the offense most often committed by adults.

According to the NHTSA, even though there was a 2 percent decline in the national crime rate during the cited period, the number of arrests for driving under the influence increased from 1.2 million in 1993 to 1.4 million in 1994—an arrest rate of one for every 127 licensed drivers in the United States. Further, approximately one-third of all drivers arrested for DWI are repeat offenders. According to the Bureau of Justice Statistics (BJS), almost nine out of ten DWI offenders in jail—86 percent—had previously been sentenced to probation, jail or prison for DWI or for other offenses.

Of the total DWI offenders sentenced to jail in 1993, the median term imposed was six months. Those offenders with two or more prior DWI sentences received sentences more than 1.3 times longer than first-time offenders.

According to the BJS, prior to their DWI arrest, one-half of the convicted offenders in jail had consumed at least six ounces of pure alcohol in the space of five hours, and approximately 29 percent had consumed at least 11 ounces of pure alcohol.

According to the FBI, arrests of youths under the age of 18 significantly increased from 1984 to 1993 for drunkenness (42.9 percent); DUI (50.2 percent); and drug abuse (27.8 percent). In addition, of all persons arrested for DUI/DWI nationally in 1993, persons in the under 25 age group accounted for 23.4 percent of those in the cities, 23.7 percent of those in the suburban counties, and 22.1 percent of those in rural counties.

Drinking and Driving Among High School Seniors

Patrick M. O'Malley and Lloyd D. Johnston

In the following selection, Patrick M. O'Malley and Lloyd D. Johnston examine attitudes toward drinking and driving among high school seniors by reviewing the questionnaire responses of approximately seventeen thousand students across the country from 1984 to 1997. The questionnaire not only asked the students about their drinking and driving behavior but also contained questions designed to determine demographic and lifestyle factors that might influence their attitudes toward drinking and driving. O'Malley and Johnston discovered that the number of students who reported driving while drunk or riding with an impaired driver declined between 1984 and 1995. However, they report, this decline has since leveled off. According to the authors, factors such as gender, ethnicity, and geographic region affect teens' drinking and driving behavior; while religious commitment, peer approval, and state laws and policies influence their attitudes toward drunk driving. O'Malley and Johnston are senior research scientists at the Institute for Social Research at the University of Michigan in Ann Arbor.

Few issues are more important to the morbidity and mortality of older adolescents and young adults than the combination of drinking and driving. Motor vehicle crashes, many of which are alcohol related, account for a very high percentage of injuries and deaths among young Americans. Therefore, information on the prevalence of, and trends in, driving after drinking and riding in a car with a driver who has been drinking is of considerable importance to the nation's public health agenda. This article uses a unique resource—the Monitoring the Future project—to provide national estimates of America's high school seniors' frequency of driving after drinking and riding with a driver who has been drinking; the information is based on self-report procedures. In addition, we report on the prevalence of such behaviors in various important demographic subgroups. We also examine the associations between driving and drinking and other factors, including religious commitment, high school grades, truancy, illicit drug use, number of evenings out per week, and miles driven in an average week.

Several of these lifestyle factors could influence the mere opportunity to drink and drive. For example, being out many evenings per week could lead to more opportunities for drinking and driving and for being a passenger in a car with a driver who has been drinking. Changes in drinking and driving could potentially be explained by changes in any of the lifestyle factors or by combinations thereof. . . .

The Questionnaire

We provide a brief overview of the Monitoring the Future study design. Nationally representative samples of about 17,000 12th graders, located in about 135 schools, were selected each year from 1975 to 1997 through a multistage scientific sampling procedure. Confidential, self-completed questionnaires were administered by professional interviewers during school hours, usually in a regularly scheduled class period. The questions on driving and drinking were added in 1984 and are included in only 1 of 6 forms (distributed in a random sequence within the classroom), so responses to these questions are based on a random one-sixth of the total sample of seniors.

The drinking and driving questions were "During the last 2 weeks, how many times (if any) have you driven a car, truck, or motorcycle after drinking alcohol?" and ". . . after having 5 or more drinks in a row?" For riding with a driver who has been drinking, the questions were "During the last 2 weeks, how many times (if any) have you been a passenger in a car when the driver has been drinking?" and ". . . when you think the driver had 5 or more drinks?" Perceived friends' disapproval was assessed by asking "How do you think your close friends feel (or would feel) about you doing each of the following things: driving a car after having 1–2 drinks and driving a car after having 5 or more drinks?"

Respondents were asked about the level of education achieved by each of their parents; responses ranged from grade school or less to graduate work. Religious commitment was a mean of 2 items assessing importance of religion in the respondent's life and frequency of attendance at religious services. Grades were assessed by the following question: "Which of the following best describes your average grade so far in high school?" Truancy was a mean of 2 measures, the frequency of skipping either classes or whole days of school during the past 4 weeks. The index of illicit drug use was a measure reflecting any use in the past 12 months of any of 9 classes of illicit drugs; respondents were classified as nonusers, users of marijuana only, or users of an illicit drug other than marijuana. Evenings out per week was assessed by asking "During a typical week, on how many evenings do you go out for fun and recreation?" Miles driven per week was assessed by asking "During an average week, how much do you usually drive a car, truck, or motorcycle?". . .

Examining the Data

Three findings were noteworthy: (1) a very large number of students have exposed themselves to alcohol-impaired driving, even at the low points; (2) a substantial improvement occurred between 1984 and 1995, most of which had occurred by 1992; and (3) no further improvement (and perhaps some relapse) occurred between 1995 and 1997.

Multivariate analyses incorporating demographic and lifestyle factors showed the following results. With respect to demographic factors, (1) male high school seniors were significantly more likely than female seniors to report driving after drinking but not to report riding with a driver who had been drinking; (2) seniors in the Northeast and West were less likely than seniors in the South and the North Central region to report alcohol-related driving or riding; (3) seniors in more rural areas reported more alcohol-involved driving or riding than did seniors in metropolitan statistical areas; (4) no significant differences were associated with parental education, a proxy for socioeconomic status; and (5) Hispanic seniors reported more riding with a driver who had been drinking, compared with White and African American seniors. With respect to lifestyle factors, (1) high school grades were not significantly associated with alcohol-related driving or riding; (2) seniors who had high levels of religious commitment reported less alcohol-associated driving or riding than did seniors who had lower levels of religious commitment; (3) truancy, use of illicit drugs, and evenings out per week all were significantly and positively related to driving after drinking and to riding with a driver who had been drinking; and (4) the number of miles driven in an average week was positively associated with driving after drinking but not with riding with a driver who had been drinking.

One of the most important conclusions of this study is that this class of adolescent risk behavior—drinking and driving—can be changed over time, as illustrated by the substantial declines in drinking and driving that occurred between 1984 and 1992. Changes in the amount of drinking account for some of the changes in drinking and driving, but the drinking-and-driving rates have decreased considerably more than drinking has. The prevalence of heavy drinking declined by about 21% between 1984 and 1997 (prevalence decreased from 39% to 31%), whereas driving after drinking and after heavy drinking both declined by about 40% over the same interval (prevalence decreased from 31% to 18% and from 18% to 11%, respectively). Furthermore, the trends in driving after drinking and after heavy drinking among only seniors who report current drinking are essentially parallel to the trends for all seniors. Another potentially important explanatory factor is the amount of driving that seniors do, but this cannot account for the declines in drinking and driving because driving has actually increased.

Attitudes Toward Drinking and Driving

Perceived risk of harm from use and disapproval of use have been important factors in explaining trends in illegal drug use. Measures of the perceived risk of harm from drinking and driving, or of seniors' own disapproval of drinking and driving, were not included in this study. However, measures of seniors' perceptions of the extent to which their friends would disapprove of their driving after drinking were available. In 1997, about half of seniors reported that their friends would strongly disapprove of their driving after having 1 to 2 drinks; in 1984, only 30% of seniors reported that level of disapproval. Between 1984 and 1997, changes in friends' disapproval of driving after drinking and in seniors' driving after drinking corresponded closely. As disapproval increased (or decreased), drinking and driving decreased (or increased). Although the close connection does not conclusively demonstrate a causal relationship, it does suggest that the substantial decline in drinking and driving observed between 1984 and 1997 may have occurred largely because of a substantial change in the social acceptability of such behavior among young people themselves.

Other factors may have contributed to reducing driving after drinking and drinking per se. Various legal and social activities have been directed at reducing drinking and driving among adults and adolescents. Increases in the minimum drinking age, which occurred between 1984 and 1987 in several states, were followed by lowered rates of drinking among students, higher perceived risk, and more disapproval of drinking in those states. This particular policy change likely was responsible for some, but certainly not all, of the decline in drinking and driving, because changes occurred in states that did not alter their minimum drinking age. Other policy initiatives aimed at youth, including "zero tolerance" laws (lower legal blood alcohol concentration limits for underage drinkers), may have played some role in the downturn.

National campaigns aimed at discouraging drunk driving by organizations such as Mothers Against Drunk Driving and the Ad Council also may have had an effect. Certainly, the hardening of peer norms against drunk driving would be consistent with such an interpretation.

The rate of alcohol-related traffic fatalities declined substantially between 1984 and 1992; the rate of decline slowed noticeably after 1992. These trends correspond closely with the observed declines in self-reported drinking and driving by high school seniors. Both indicators accord with broader societal events, including the substantial national attention given to the Mothers Against Drunk Driving efforts (which peaked around 1984), the increases in minimum drinking ages (which occurred primarily between 1984 and 1987), and the national campaign for "designated drivers" (which occurred primarily between 1989 and 1992). Societal attention to, and media coverage of, drinking and driving has abated since then, and we may be seeing the results of that abatement.

The recent leveling and, perhaps, upturn in rates of driving after drinking by students provide cause for concern. A process of "generational forgetting" of the dangers of drugs may be responsible for the upturn in illicit drug use observed in the early 1990s; that is, the more recent cohorts of teenagers have heard and seen considerably less of the dangers of drugs than earlier cohorts heard and saw. A similar process may be occurring with respect to the dangers of driving after drinking. If so, new prevention efforts may be necessary, including policy initiatives and systematic media campaigns, to avert a relapse in driving after drinking among newer cohorts of teenagers.

HELL ON WHEELS: THE HARD-CORE DRUNK DRIVER

Bill Hewitt

Despite the decrease in drunk driving fatalities since 1982, hard-core drunk drivers—repeat offenders who often have extremely high blood alcohol levels—continue to injure and kill people across the United States. In the following article, Bill Hewitt explains that hard-core drunk drivers frequently ignore or circumvent the laws designed to keep them off the road. For example, Hewitt describes the case of a convicted drunk driver who had been given a week to settle his affairs before serving time in jail; during that week, the man again drove while drunk and caused an accident in which three people lost their lives. According to Hewitt, many hard-core drunk drivers fail all attempts at rehabilitation and continue to break the law unless they are incarcerated. Hewitt is a senior writer for *People* magazine.

Of all the social ills that bedevil us, drunk driving is one we seem to be able to do something about. Thanks to increased public awareness, stiffer penalties and higher drinking ages—not to mention air bags and greater use of seat belts—the number of fatalities caused by drinking and driving has dropped sharply over the past decade. In 1982 more than 25,000 people were killed in alcohol-related car accidents. Last year [1993], that number was down more than 30 percent, to just over 17,000.

Yet while the number of deaths has diminished, a troubling problem remains. Government and law-enforcement officials see a worrisome percentage of accidents caused by a hard core of repeat offenders, many of whom have multiple arrests for driving under the influence. "The incorrigible driver is where the major problem lies," says James B. Jacobs, a New York University law professor and the author of the study *Drunk Driving*. "They are the hardest people to control. The social drinkers are the ones who listen to the television ads."

Although nationwide statistics are not available on repeat offender drunk drivers, individual states have compiled their own sobering figures. In Ohio, for instance, 32 percent of drunken drivers are repeaters,

Reprinted, with permission, from Bill Hewitt, "Hell on Wheels," *People Weekly*, October 17, 1994.

and they are responsible for 55 percent of all drunk driving convictions. In recent years a host of remedies aimed at such hard-core drunks have been tried, from strict alcohol-treatment programs to devices that require a driver to pass a Breathalyzer test before his car will start. Lately popular sentiment has seemed to favor longer prison sentences for repeat offenders. As the following cases suggest, however, simple solutions are elusive. The frightening truth is that drunk drivers are deadly—and often utterly heedless of society's sanctions.

Turning a Drinker into a Killer

Circuit court Judge Peter Dearing thought he had made an impression on Keith Jones. In June 1992, Jones, then 31, a landscaper from Jacksonville, Fla., had pleaded guilty to driving under the influence after he had rear-ended another car. It was the second time that Jones had been arrested for drunk driving, so Judge Dearing, known for meting out tough punishment, sentenced him to 90 days in jail.

As part of Jones's plea bargain, Judge Dearing gave him a week to get his personal affairs in order before starting to serve his time. But just three days before his sentence was to begin, Jones was out drinking with a friend. The two met Sandy Johnson at a bar, and shortly after 1 A.M. on June 7 [1992], offered to give her a ride home. As they traveled along Jacksonville's Atlantic Boulevard in Jones's red Toyota pickup, Jones and Johnson got into an argument about where to make a turnoff. When Jones tried to make an abrupt turn too quickly, he swung wide and veered into oncoming traffic. The truck hit a Ford Crown Victoria driven by Arthur DeLoach, 73, who had been out dancing at a local Moose Lodge with his wife, Virginia, 69, and their friends Guerry and Earleen Joiner. The collision killed both DeLoaches and Guerry Joiner, 61. Jones, who suffered minor injuries, climbed out of his truck and left the scene. Arrested shortly after the accident, he eventually pleaded guilty to multiple counts of motor-vehicle homicide and received a 20-year sentence, of which he will probably end up serving 12.

While acknowledging he had several beers that night, Jones insists that alcohol had nothing to do with the accident. "I was definitely not impaired," he says, though the alcohol level in his blood was measured at .19 percent, nearly double the legal level for intoxication, which was .10 in Florida at the time and is .08 now. In his view, the whole tragedy should be chalked up to bad luck. And while he readily voices regret for the victims and their families, he is inclined to see himself as a victim as well. "I had it made, and I blew it all for a simple mistake," he says. "I didn't go out to hurt anybody. I'm not a bad person."

All the same, former assistant state attorney Wayne Ellis, who prosecuted the case, left little to chance. If Jones should violate the terms of his 15-year probation once he gets out, by either drinking or driving, he will go straight back to prison, perhaps for as much as another

27 years. One way or another "the public has been protected," says Ellis, now in private practice. Perhaps so, says Barry Sweedler of the National Transportation Safety Board, but there is a limit to the number of repeat offenders who can be put away for long stretches. "You can't put these people in jail, except for the egregious cases," he says. "There's no room in the jails." For his part, Jones vows that when he is once again a free man, he will buy a limousine and hire a chauffeur to drive him around.

A Driver Wipes Out a Family

When it came to his family's safety, Giovanni Vaccarello, a retired machinist from New York City's borough of Brooklyn, never took anything for granted. He often drove his daughters Maria, 18, and Concetta, 17, to their part-time jobs. He insisted that his son John, now 14, wear a beeper so he was never out of touch. He routinely walked his wife of nearly 25 years, Cathy, 45, the one block from their home to her job in a beauty salon. "I was afraid," says Giovanni, 51. "I didn't want anything to happen to them."

Yet none of his precautions could protect his family from Abraham Myers, [then] a 55-year-old janitor. Around 11:40 P.M. on May 1 [1994], Vaccarello left the Russo's on the Bay catering hall in Queens with Cathy, Maria and Concetta. John remained behind as the rest of the family began to walk across the street to their car. Meanwhile, Myers, allegedly going more than 70 mph with the headlights of his 1982 Lincoln Continental turned off, ran a red light and slammed into them, scattering the Vaccarellos like duck pins. The impact hurled Giovanni and Concetta into the air. Maria hit the front windshield and was carried 150 feet, and Cathy was dragged 180 feet before Myers' car came to a stop. She and Maria died instantly. Concetta lingered for a few hours on life support before dying. Giovanni's left leg was broken in three places, and he suffered a heart attack, which required more than a month of hospitalization. "If he came at me with a gun, I've got a chance," says Giovanni, "but not with a five-ton car."

Myers' blood alcohol was later tested at .2, double the state's legal limit for driving while intoxicated. Myers already had a previous conviction for drunk driving, and dating back to 1967, his license had been suspended 26 times. Not that Myers probably cared—he continued driving without a valid license. Despite that clear record of recklessness and disregard for the law, he had never served a day in prison. Finally that may change. Now awaiting trial on charges including murder, manslaughter, vehicular manslaughter and driving under the influence of alcohol, Myers faces up to life in prison if convicted. That, of course, is no consolation to Giovanni, who feels only hatred for Myers. "I wonder if he sleeps," says Giovanni bitterly. "Not only did he kill them, he made a mess out of them."

Acting under a New York State law passed almost a year ago [1993], police can now charge with a felony those caught driving without a valid license if they've had 10 or more license suspensions. "Driving without a license really has to be taken as a serious offense," says safety expert Barry Sweedler. "Right now, it's just a slap on the wrist." Indeed, in just the first six months of 1994, some 5,589 people were arrested in New York City for driving with suspended licenses.

A Blind Spot in the System Proves Fatal

It was 9:30 A.M. on Aug. 2 [1994], and Michael Graham, 36, who ferried elderly and disabled passengers in a van for the regional transit authority in Philadelphia, notified his dispatcher that he had made his last run of the morning. What he did for several hours afterward is unclear. But the next thing anyone knew, Graham was at the wheel of his empty van at 2:30 P.M.—legally drunk according to police—and smashing across the median barrier on Interstate 95 North in Philadelphia. Soaring over two lanes of oncoming traffic, he landed on top of a 1992 Mitsubishi Eclipse, shearing off its roof.

Inside were Kelly Sweeney, 26, a nurse, and her sister Cassie, 23, a student teacher, both of Pennsauken, N.J., who were on their way home from a dress fitting for a cousin's wedding. The impact killed Cassie and severely injured Kelly, who suffered serious brain and head injuries (both her ears were sheared off). Ten weeks later the victims' parents, Dennis and Catherine Sweeney, still cannot fathom the utter capricious horror of what has happened to their family. Local transit officials were shocked by the collision as well, especially after discovering that, unknown to them, Graham had compiled an appalling driving record.

Police learned, for instance, that Graham, using the alias James Mason, was wanted on bench warrants stemming from two DUI [driving under the influence] arrests in 1991. (He also had convictions on drug charges and for firearms possession and auto theft.) Just last July [1994] he had been arrested for DUI twice under his own name within three weeks. Why would anyone risk serious injury or criminal prosecution over and over again? "A lot of times a driver will drink and nothing bad happens to them, so it makes it easier the next time," says Tom Culpepper, a safety expert for the American Automobile Association. "The more you do it, the easier it is not to think about the possible consequences."

To get his job, Graham had gone through a three-month screening process that included a drug and alcohol test and a background check of convictions. The trouble, says Carol Lavoritano, the official in charge of Philadelphia's Paratransit network, is that in too many cases red flags don't show up in such reviews. Prospective employers have access only to court records of convictions, which, because of plea bargains and provisions for expunging offenses after a certain period, are often incomplete or misleading. They do not have access to arrest records, which give a clearer indication of potentially unsuitable employees. Even now, sitting in the Philadelphia Detention Center and facing a possible 30 years if found guilty of all charges, including vehicular homicide while intoxicated, Graham could conceivably apply for another driving job and not set off any alarms since he has yet to be convicted of anything. "To this day, Michael Graham has a clean driver's license," says Lavoritano. "If you ordered it up today, none of this would appear."

The Revolving Door of Rehab

Around the Gentner Communications Corp. in Salt Lake City [Utah], Paul Bredehoft, 39, was known as a model employee. In the two years he worked at the plant, he almost never failed to show up for his 7 A.M. shift assembling teleconferencing equipment. "He came in, quietly did his job each day and left," says manufacturing manager Mike Slaugh. "He never discussed his personal life." Bredehoft's reliability was remarkable considering that he apparently spent many of his off-hours pounding down one beer after another. "I'd see him sitting on the front porch of his apartment, drinking beer all day," says neighbor Jordan Dew. "Drinking was his main pastime."

And, it would appear, his fatal flaw. Beginning 10 years ago [in 1984], Bredehoft was convicted six times of drunk driving. But in contrast to many repeat offenders, Bredehoft didn't slip through any bureaucratic cracks. In fact his experience provides a depressing illustration of the limitations of the criminal justice system even when it does work.

After his very first drunk driving conviction, in November 1984, he had his license suspended and was sentenced to six months in jail. When Bredehoft agreed to complete an in-patient alcohol-recovery program, his jail term was suspended. Less than three years later, though, he was busted again for DUI, which led to yet another in-patient treatment program. In 1989 and 1990, after three more arrests, Salt Lake County Court Judge Phyllis Scott sentenced him to six months in jail or further in-patient treatment. "I don't see how you can be more harsh than I was," says Judge Scott. "I gave him the maximum sentence under the law."

While endorsing the need for rehab programs, many experts caution that they are far from cure-alls. "Most programs can only boast a 50 percent success rate, if that," says Earl W. Patterson, a professor and substance abuse authority at Nova Southeastern University in Fort Lauderdale [Florida]. "Remember, you're not only changing a particular habit, often it's a lifestyle as well." Thus it shouldn't have been surprising when Bredehoft was arrested again in August 1993 for DUI. This time he spent 10 days in jail and participated in DUI education classes and group counseling at Alcoholics Anonymous, both 12-week programs.

Any hope that he had finally kicked his habit of drinking and driving came to a horrific end a few months later. At 7:30 P.M. on March 1

[1994], 17-year-old Sean Adkins and six of his friends were stopped in the emergency lane of Interstate 15 in Salt Lake City trying to fix a flat tire. According to police, Bredehoft was legally drunk and doing 60 mph in his red Mustang when he hit Sean, who was standing by the side of the road, and plowed into the disabled car. Sean's friends all escaped serious injury, but Sean, an honor student at Highland High School, was killed almost instantly.

Found guilty on Sept. 7 [1994], of second-degree felony automobile homicide while intoxicated, Bredehoft could be sentenced to 15 years in prison. Even that wouldn't satisfy Sean's 20-year-old brother Brad. "I don't know if there is any just punishment for what he did," says Brad. "Life in prison isn't enough. I don't know what is." Sean's father, Michael, an attorney, is certain now what measures society *shouldn't* bother to take in dealing with hard-core drunk drivers—namely, trying to cure them. "Bredehoft should never be out of jail," he says. "The reality is, we can't send messages to drunks."

DRUNK DRIVING MAKES A COMEBACK

Paula Spencer

In the following selection, Paula Spencer discusses the growing concern over the recent trends in drunk driving in the United States. As a result of changing social attitudes toward drunk driving in the 1980s and early 1990s, new laws were implemented that significantly reduced the number of alcohol-related fatalities, Spencer writes. However, she reveals, drunk driving activists fear that both legislators and the public have become complacent about drunk driving, considering it an issue that has largely been solved. Unfortunately, Spencer explains, in the mid-1990s, the number of alcohol-related fatalities and drunk driving arrests began to rise while few new laws were passed. Most advocates of stricter policies believe that as long as there are victims of drunk driving, the fight against drunk driving is not over, she reports. Spencer is a contributing editor to *Woman's Day* magazine.

Even before she was born, Kara Hensel was a drunk-driving victim.

After her seven-months-pregnant mother was burned over 73 percent of her body in a car crash in 1971, Kara was delivered by emergency cesarean section. Because of her prematurity she was legally blind. Her mom, fighting for her own life, didn't meet her scrappy newborn until Kara was 11 days old. She remained physically unable to hold her daughter until her first birthday. Worst of all, Kara never met her big sister Lori Lynn, then 4, and her 19-month-old cousin Mitch Pewitt, who lived next door. They were killed in the same wreck.

"Only they didn't call it drunk driving back then," says Kara's mom Millie Webb, who lives near Kara in Franklin, Tennessee, with her husband, Roy, who was also severely burned that day, and their youngest daughter Ashlea. It was no crime in 1971 to drive under the influence of alcohol. The 17-year-old neighbor who rear-ended the Webbs' Chevy on a bridge just three miles from home, causing it to explode on impact, received two months' probation for vehicular homicide.

Reprinted, with permission, from Paula Spencer, "Drunk Driving: The Menace Is Back," *Woman's Day*, March 31, 1997.

Changing Attitudes

Since the tragedy that smashed her life to bits, Millie Webb has seen social attitudes toward driving drunk make a 180-degree turn. More than 2,000 new laws were enacted in the 1980s and early 1990s to help deter and punish those who drive while intoxicated (DWI). The number of alcohol-related fatal crashes dropped from more than 25,000 in 1982 to 16,580 in 1994. Nevertheless, Millie was startled recently when a former highway-safety activist told her, "Oh, drinking and driving is an old issue nowadays."

Thinking of her three months in the Vanderbilt University Medical Center burn unit in Nashville, Tennessee, every salty tear further searing her face as she mourned her daughters—one dead, one blinded—and her infant nephew, Millie looked the woman squarely in the face. "I deal every day with parents who hurt like I hurt when my Lori was killed. We've come a long way, but we still have a long way to go."

Unfortunately, many activists and experts *do* fear that the war against drunk driving—one of the biggest public-health success stories in America—may be stalling out. Consider:

- In 1995, the most recent year for which figures are available, the number of alcohol-related traffic fatalities went up to 17,274, reversing almost two decades of steady decline.
- The consumption of beer, which is involved in more than three-fourths of such crashes, is leveling off after years of gradual decline.
- Few new laws targeting the drunk driver passed, especially ones aimed at the 25-to-50 age group—representative of the majority of the drivers on the road today.
- Nationwide, DWI arrests are up, but so are violations. In many communities, DWI charges never translate into convictions or stiff sentences, thanks to overloaded dockets and a there-but-for-the-grace-of-God-go-I reluctance of judges and juries.

Is Drunk Driving an Old Issue?

These days, says Katherine Prescott, the former national president of Mothers Against Drunk Driving (MADD), in Irving, Texas, "the number-one problem is complacency." In 1996, the group gave the U.S. a grade of C in its progress on the issue, down from B-minus just three years earlier. "People assume the problem is already solved, or well on its way," says Prescott, whose own 16-year-old son, Jay, was killed by a repeat offender in 1981.

Legislators have wearied of the issue too, Prescott charges. "Their perception is, 'Those MADD people are here again? Haven't we done all we need to do?'"

In part, the grassroots groups that formed in the late 1970s to spearhead a national campaign against driving drunk are a victim of their own success. By the mid-1980s, national organizations like Remove Intoxicated Drivers (RID-USA) and MADD grew more than 450 local chapters, says John McCarthy, Ph.D., a sociologist at Catholic University in Washington, D.C., who has studied the citizen-action movement against drunk driving. This victim involvement helped channel outrage into action in a way that the government alone could not, he says—elevating the highway carnage to center stage in the public eye.

Today, though, fresher horrors grab headlines, like tales of gun-toting 11-year-olds and flesh-eating bacteria strains. Often people perceive air bag and airplane safety as more urgent transportation problems, even though they cause a fraction as many deaths.

In addition, police, prosecutors and jails are being asked to do more with fewer resources, experts say, making enforcement of existing laws tougher.

The Problem of Teen Drinking

According to Jim Fell, chief of research and evaluation in traffic safety programs for the National Highway Traffic Safety Administration (NHTSA), the good news, if any, in the upturn in drunk-driving deaths, lies in what the statistics *didn't* show: a decline in the involvement of teenagers—a group of drivers typically twice as involved in drunk-driving accidents as those over 21. That's the direct result of policies aimed at this age group. NHTSA credits the raising of the drinking age to 21 with preventing some 1,000 deaths a year. What's more, 37 states—17 of them between 1994 and 1995 alone—have passed "zero-tolerance" laws providing for the immediate suspension of the license of any driver under 21 found with any measurable amount of alcohol in his or her system. States with such laws have been shown to reduce drunk-driving fatalities by one-fifth.

But one-fifth, advocates say, is still not low enough. Not as long as there are people like Kimberly Peacock of Griffin, Georgia, who has twice been the victim of drunk drivers. The first time it was just Kimberly's car that was wrecked; the second time her whole life was shattered.

At dinnertime on December 20, 1995, Kimberly's fiancé, David Harris, Jr., offered to drive her twin sons, Daniel and Zachary, and her daughter, Virginia, to their father's house on his way to work. Because Kimberly was nine months pregnant, David wanted her to stay at home and rest. En route, David picked up a coworker, Dana Ogletree. While making a left turn on a familiar highway, the car was broadsided by a drunk and high 17-year-old who crossed the center yellow line.

The teen driver sustained only cuts and bruises. But all five in the Harris car were killed: David; father of five Dana Ogletree; 7-year-old Virginia; and the twin boys, who would have turned 9 the next day. Kimberly's daughter, Asia Harris, was born three days after the accident, the same day her father was buried. "This doesn't just affect me—my daughter has to grow up without a father or siblings," says Kimberly, 28. "There are grandparents, cousins, teachers, neighbors, schoolmates and friends who mourn, too."

INTERNATIONAL TRENDS IN DRINKING AND DRIVING

R. Jean Wilson

Since the early 1980s, the United States, Canada, and several other nations have experienced a decline in the number of alcohol-related traffic fatalities. However, R. Jean Wilson writes in the following article, the rates of and the reasons for this decline vary from country to country. Wilson compares the drunk driving trends in various countries, including differences in blood alcohol concentration (BAC) limits, the severity of drunk driving laws, and the percentage of drivers who are discovered to be over the legal BAC limits. According to the author, most of these countries have responded to the problem of drunk driving in similar ways; therefore, the variance in the rate of decline may result from national differences in customs and attitudes toward the government and law enforcement agencies. Wilson is the director of research and evaluation at the Motor Vehicle Branch of the Ministry of the Attorney General, Victoria, British Columbia, Canada.

In North America, the 1980's have been hailed by people interested in traffic safety as the decade of progress, particularly with respect to reductions in alcohol-related casualties. The period was characterized by a "get-tough" approach to legislation and enforcement aimed at drinking-driving, typified by the U.S. Presidential Commission on Drunk Driving and the Canadian Bill C-19 amendments to the Criminal Code that introduced harsher penalties for drinking-driving. There was also an increase in public education and public awareness campaigns, heightened media attention, rising public moral indignation, and general consciousness-raising initiated for drinking-driving at both the government and the grassroots levels.

In tandem with these developments were policies for stricter control over the advertising, consumption, and distribution of alcohol, particularly in the United States (e.g., minimum legal drinking age laws, controls over alcoholic beverage pricing and hours of sale, increased taxation on alcoholic beverages, and provision of warning

Excerpted from "Drinking and Driving: In Search of Solutions to an International Problem," by R. Jean Wilson, *Alcohol Health and Research World*, vol. 17, no. 3 (1993), a publication of the U.S. government. References in the original have been omitted here but are available from the author.

labels on alcoholic beverage containers). Many or all of these factors have been cited as possible contributors to the reductions observed in alcohol-related motor vehicle fatalities. However, there is no clear evidence that any one or combination of these factors is causally related to the observed decline. Indeed, economic factors such as the recession and unemployment have undoubtedly played a contributory role, because they are associated with both reduced driving and reduced alcohol consumption. Unfortunately, it is difficult to estimate the magnitude of this role relative to other factors.

The decline in drinking-driving fatalities began in the early 1980's and has continued into the 1990's, although perhaps at a decelerated rate. Some observers have noted a declining momentum of drinking-driving initiatives and abating interest on the part of the media and the public. As H.M. Simpson states:

> At least in North America a plateau appears to have been reached in the level of importance attached to the drinking-driving issue; partly because the intensity of concern evidenced in the early 1980's simply could not be sustained and partly because other issues, such as AIDS and illicit drug use, have entered the social agenda to compete with the drinking-driving issue.

Global Trends in Drunk Driving

A decline in alcohol-related traffic casualties is not limited to Canada and the United States. Similar trends have been recorded in several countries, including Australia, Finland, the Netherlands, and the United Kingdom, although methods of measuring the trends have varied in different countries.

Researchers most often assess yearly drinking-driving trends using the proportion of fatally injured drivers with blood alcohol concentrations (BAC's) greater than some specified level. The specified level may equal the legal BAC limit of the country or be set as low as trace levels of alcohol, depending on the report or the researcher. The Australian States also assess drinking-driving trends using recorded BAC's of drivers admitted to hospitals as a result of motor vehicle crashes—a provision made possible by legislation. To assess drinking-driving trends, some countries, such as the Netherlands, rely on police reports of alcohol involvement in crashes; these reports tend to underestimate frequency of alcohol involvement but still can be used to assess trends over time. Although there are variations for each country in terms of the year when the decline in drinking-driving casualties started and the extent of stabilization, the downward trend is consistent among all the countries for which data are available.

Although accident statistics provide a measure of the consequences of drinking-driving, roadside surveys of the BAC's obtained from breath samples of randomly stopped motorists (i.e., random breath tests [RBT's]) provide an estimate of the extent of drinking-driving. Such surveys have been conducted periodically by several countries and generally have revealed declining trends. In Finland, annual RBT surveys have shown reductions in drinking-driving of more than 50 percent between 1979 and 1985 in the number of motorists with positive BAC's; however, in the early 1990's, the proportion of drinking-drivers has been increasing slightly, rather than declining.

Roadside surveys conducted in the Netherlands since 1970 have demonstrated a decrease of about 50 percent in the proportion of weekend nighttime drivers over the legal BAC limit (0.05 percent) between 1983 and 1988. Over a similar period in South Australia, roadside surveys showed evidence of declines in drinking-driving.

M.B. Biecheler-Fretel and C. Filou report that between 1985 and 1991, on rural roads in two *départements,* or counties, in France there was an overall increase in the percentage of drivers having consumed any alcohol, no change in the percentage of drivers over the legal limit (0.08 percent), and a slight decrease in the proportion of drinking-drivers at higher BAC's (exceeding 0.15 percent). In Canada, small but significant reductions in the proportion of drivers over the legal BAC limit (0.08 percent) were found between 1974 and 1986 in three Provinces. . . .

Comparisons Among Countries

Roadside survey results reveal vast differences in the proportion of nighttime drinking-drivers in various countries. The following examples were selected on the basis of comparability of sampling hours, although there may be some differences between countries in sampling procedures. The Nordic countries (Finland, Norway, and Sweden) have achieved remarkably low levels of drinking-driving—typically around 1 percent of nighttime drivers have BAC's higher than 0.05 percent. This level can be compared with the most recent results for other countries: the United States, 8.4 percent; Great Britain, approximately 3 percent; the Netherlands, 4 percent; France, 5 percent on rural roads in one region only; and Canada, 5 to 8 percent, depending on the Province. The Nordic countries also differ from other countries in having lower BAC limits, strict alcohol control policies, traditionally severe sanctions for driving-while-intoxicated (DWI) offenses (particularly in Norway), and rigorous enforcement of drinking-driving legislation using RBT.

Although the Nordic countries appear to have achieved a relative degree of control over drinking-driving, those drivers who do drink and drive tend to be problem drinkers who are alcohol dependent or who regularly drink and have high BAC's. Experts in the Nordic countries concede that the easiest gains in traffic safety have been made through deterrence of nonproblem drinkers. These experts emphasize that efforts must now focus on the less deterrable drinking-drivers: high alcohol consumers, problem drinkers, and DWI recidivists. Indeed, as we shall see in the next section, these so-called hardcore drinking-drivers have been identified as contributing disproportionately to the alcohol-traffic safety problem in all countries where research data are available.

The Hard-core Drunk Driver

There is a growing concern worldwide over those who drive with high BAC's and who are at elevated risk of crash involvement. The basis for this concern comes from several sources. In the United States, fatally injured drinking-drivers account for more than 40 percent of drivers killed each year; among those drinking-drivers, 64 percent have BAC's of more than 0.15 percent and 40 percent have BAC's of more than 0.20 percent, resulting in a mean BAC among fatally injured drinking-drivers of 0.17 percent. A similar BAC distribution is found in countries such as Australia, Canada, Finland, Great Britain, and Sweden.

Increasing evidence exists that drivers with prior DWI convictions make up a higher proportion of drivers killed in fatal crashes than was previously believed. Although fatality data from the United States show that only 14 percent of fatally injured drinking-drivers have previous DWI convictions, this is likely an underestimate due to the fallibility of record-keeping systems; many States purge driving records every 5 to 10 years, thereby erasing older convictions and underestimating recidivism rates. In Minnesota, where it is possible to accurately identify those arrested or charged with drinking-driving since 1976, almost 35 percent of alcohol-related fatal crashes were found to involve a driver with a prior DWI offense.

High BAC's have been found to dominate among drivers arrested and convicted of drinking-driving in several countries, despite varying legal BAC limits. The mean BAC of convicted drinking-drivers in countries with published data ranges from 0.15 percent to 0.18 percent. This high mean BAC could reflect that arrests and convictions depend on detection, and the chances of detecting a drinking-driver increase at higher BAC's where impairment is more visible (e.g., swerving, speeding, and reckless driving). In countries that use the RBT, drivers detected through RBT have lower BAC's, on average, than do drivers detected through routine patrols, because RBT provides a "net" for drivers over a broader BAC distribution, whereas routine patrols detect mainly the high BAC drivers. H.M. Simpson and D.R. Mayhew argue that enforcement systems such as RBT and sobriety checkpoints are not efficient for detecting high-BAC drivers, who should be the primary target of enforcement. Nonetheless, in Finland, 40 percent of RBT-arrested drivers showed physiological evidence of problem drinking (e.g., abnormal liver enzyme activity). The explanation proffered by J.A. Dunbar, A. Penttila, and J. Pikkarainen is that round-the-clock RBT patrols often detect problem drinkers in the morning when their BAC's have declined from the night before but are still over the legal limit.

Most countries report that a high proportion of convicted drinking-drivers are repeat offenders. Moreover, this proportion appears to be increasing. Countries with lower rates of drinking-driving, as determined by roadside surveys, tend to report higher rates of recidivism, perhaps due to the greater control over drinking-driving by the more socially compliant segment of the population. Recidivist drinking-drivers typically have higher BAC's on arrest than do first offenders, report higher levels of alcohol consumption, and have higher incidences of alcohol problems and alcoholism. Furthermore, a high BAC on a first arrest is predictive of subsequent arrests.

Responding to Drunk Driving Trends

The recent focus on the hardcore drinking-driver has led many researchers and practitioners in the alcohol and driving field to recognize that drinking-driving deterrence and intervention policies must be adapted to address the problems presented by these high-risk people. As stated by Simpson and Mayhew: "An effective countermeasure strategy aimed at the problem of high-BAC drivers will need to embrace a variety of tactics including primary, secondary, and tertiary prevention programs.". . .

There has been a certain commonality in how countries have responded to drinking-driving since the early 1980's. Most countries for which data are available report declining levels of drinking-driving and/or alcohol involvement in fatal motor vehicle crashes during the 1980's, with decelerating rates of decline in more recent years. The reasons for the decline are not well understood and vary by country— the Nordic countries have achieved remarkably low levels of drinking-driving, whereas countries such as the United States and Canada have higher levels—but it is generally believed that deterrent approaches in the form of new legislation and modified enforcement practices have played a significant role. Although they are recognizing the need to maintain general deterrence, many countries are now focusing research and prevention efforts on the more intractable hardcore, high-BAC driver. As many as 35 percent of drinking-drivers involved in fatal crashes have previous drinking-driving convictions, emphasizing the need for programs to rehabilitate offenders.

Differences between countries in their approach to drinking-driving often can be linked to differences in social norms, customs, and practices. Attitudes toward laws, government control, and individual rights and freedoms; attitudes of the police; the role of alcohol in society; and the role of the private automobile can influence whether a drinking-driving countermeasure is acceptable. For example, a minimum drinking age law of 21, so readily adopted in the United States, would be difficult to implement in many European countries in which adolescent's traditionally drink, particularly with their families at meals. Similarly, RBT as practiced in Australia and Scandinavia is unlikely to be adopted (at least within the twentieth century) in Canada, Great Britain, or the United States because of constitutional barriers and attitudes toward individual rights. As Simpson has pointed out, importing drinking-driving countermeasures without regard for the social context will compromise their impact; the way in which administrators and recipients view countermeasures determines their viability.

The international transfer of knowledge and information is essential to drinking-driving control efforts. Lessons learned from other countries serve to minimize redundant research and facilitate the implementation of new drinking-driving countermeasures. Commonalities in the drinking-driving problem far outweigh international differences; recognition and open discussion of these differences will foster understanding of the problem and its interaction with the social, cultural, and political environment.

CHAPTER 2

PERSONAL STORIES OF TRAGEDY AND TRIUMPH

A Young Life Forever Changed

Lisa Wright

In the following article, Lisa Wright, a teenager from Birch Run, Michigan, tells the story of how her "pretty normal" life changed forever one night when she was ejected from a car driven by a drunk driver. Lisa explains that she, her boyfriend, and several friends had been having a party in the car with alcohol her boyfriend had purchased with a fake ID. Lisa was the only one hurt seriously in the accident. She describes the difficulty of discovering that she would never walk again, seeing the scars on her face for the first time, and beginning the long process of rehabilitation. Although Lisa says she has learned a valuable lesson about not taking life for granted, she still regrets the accident and advises people not to drink and drive or to get into a car with someone who has been drinking.

I wasn't the perfect 17-year-old high school senior, but I was pretty normal. I was a cheerleader and the president of my class in Birch Run, Michigan. I was a good student. I had a lot going for me, and I was really looking forward to college.

I drank, but I wasn't the kind of person who was out drinking all the time or even every weekend. I just liked to party with my friends and have a good time. Sometimes, like a lot of kids, I did get drunk.

Joe was my boyfriend at the time. He was the kind of person who would often drink and drive. Even though I never drove drunk, I rode with him pretty often when he had been drinking, and it always seemed that everything would be OK.

He lived about an hour away, and one weekend he came up with some friends I had never met before. My girlfriend and I went driving with them, and we couldn't figure out what we wanted to do.

Cruising and Drinking

Joe had a fake ID and bought some vodka and wine coolers. The truth is Joe and his friends had been drinking before they even arrived at my house. I could smell it on Joe's breath, but I wasn't worried. It wasn't the first time. Pretty soon we all were drinking and cruising around. It got later and later, too late to really do anything like go to the movies. So we just kept drinking and cruising. We ended up about an hour and a half from my town. I think we were looking for a place to play pool or something.

Joe gave up the driver's seat to a guy named Jason. I remember sitting in the back seat on Joe's lap while Jason drove, and I recall that nobody was wearing a seat belt.

After that, I don't remember anything. The police report says that Jason took a curve in a 25 mph zone at somewhere between 80 and 90 mph. The car went off the road, hit a telephone pole, and flipped four times before stopping in a driveway.

Amazingly, nobody else was seriously hurt. But I was hurt badly—thrown straight through the back window. I was rushed to the trauma unit, and for several days the doctors didn't know if I was going to live. My lungs were badly damaged; that was the main concern. After five days or so, it was clear that I would live.

Discovering the Damage

But I was in such bad shape. I had broken a bunch of bones: my shoulder blades, my collar bone, my jaw, five of my ribs. I don't remember realizing I couldn't feel my legs. I was on so many drugs that everything seemed like a blur. It took a couple of weeks to get my head straight. Still, I do remember something was terribly wrong. I asked the doctor if I would be able to walk again, and he just looked at me and said no. I remember how cold he was. He didn't try to make it seem better than it was, and I'm glad. He made me open my eyes and face facts.

One day, a few weeks after the accident, I looked in the mirror and thought, "Oh, God, I'm a monster. I look like such a freak." I had scars on my face; my eyes were completely red. You couldn't even see the whites of my eyes. My face was swollen, my teeth had huge braces on them, and I didn't even remember the surgery on my mouth. They put a hole in my throat so I could breathe. I had tubes up my nose. It was pretty gross—and terribly painful.

For a while I thought about killing myself, but I was too sick to do anything about it. I thought my life was completely over. I thought there is no way I'm ever going to make it out of this. No one is ever going to love me. I'll never be able to get married and have kids. I thought this just can't be happening. It's not me. But it was me.

Putting a Life Back Together

Putting things back together took a long, long time. I went to a rehabilitation center in Colorado. It was really hard, and I was in a lot of pain. I had no idea what was in store for me. Learning to do the simplest things like getting dressed or putting on a pair of shoes was exhausting. In fact, I was so weak that just sitting up could make me so dizzy that I'd vomit.

In Colorado, I was miserable. I cried every day. Joe and I broke up, and that was pretty terrible. But I wanted to go home so much that I kept working super hard, lifting weights, stretching, learning to become mobile in my wheelchair. I went home after three months, even though they wanted me to stay for another month. I made it home for graduation and the senior prom.

When the thrill of returning home wore off, I felt like a stranger in my own house—like I was living someone else's life. I couldn't do a lot of things I wanted to, and I realized that three months of rehab was just the beginning.

Slowly things have gotten better. My parents and close friends have always been there for me. It's now a year and a half since the accident. I've just finished my first year of college, and I'm really excited about getting my own specially equipped van so I can drive myself. I'll be able to live on my own and take care of myself completely without having to rely on anyone else. I'm fortunate enough to have the use of my hands. There are a lot of people who can't say that.

But the truth is I'm still working to be independent. I struggle with it every day. For example, I have a boyfriend, and when I'm out somewhere (I'm always in my wheelchair), a lot of times people stare at me. That really gets him mad, but I'm learning to ignore it. In fact, most of the time I don't even realize people are staring.

Of course, there's nothing in the world I would want more than to be able to walk again. And yet, a lot of good has come out of all this. Before, I didn't really appreciate what I had. I took a lot of things and people for granted. Now, I've gained a lot of compassion for people. I appreciate life a lot more than I used to. In fact, I can't remember being this happy before.

If I could give advice to anyone about alcohol and driving, I'd say don't drink and drive—and never get in a car with someone who has been drinking. You just can't make exceptions. People think that the possibility of being in an accident is so far away—that tragedy is so distant. But when alcohol is involved, tragedy can be right around the next corner.

THE WOMEN OF MOTHERS AGAINST DRUNK DRIVING (MADD)

Joey Kennedy

In the following article, Joey Kennedy relates the stories of five members of Mothers Against Drunk Driving (MADD) who were nominated from among their own members as outstanding representatives of MADD. From all walks of life—a single parent to a Ph.D. candidate—these women describe not only their personal tragedies as the result of drunk driving but also how they decided to help other victims and work to prevent similar tragedies. Lobbying for changes in their state drunk driving laws and lecturing, training, and counseling adults and teenagers on the dangers of drunk driving, these women never give up. Many believe that only through their own efforts can they survive the devastation inflicted on their lives by the actions of drunk drivers. Joey Kennedy is a Pulitzer Prize–winning editorial writer for the *Birmingham (Ala.) News*.

The foot soldiers in the war against drunk driving are the 3.5 million volunteers, members, and supporters of Mothers Against Drunk Driving (MADD). Working at the grassroots level for no pay and little recognition, they have had tremendous impact on individuals, in their communities, and in their state legislatures. In 1997, *Redbook* asked MADD's members to nominate from their own ranks those MADD mothers they considered truly outstanding. As the nominations poured in, we read them and wept for the personal tragedies that led so many to join MADD. But we are equally moved, and inspired, by the energy and sheer grit that allowed these women to turn their grief into action—action that makes a difference for all of us. In May 1997, *Redbook* honored these five outstanding MADD mothers at a special luncheon in Washington, D.C.

Could It Happen Again?

When the telephone rings late at night, Linda Hull gets frightened.

The phone rang in March of 1987, and Linda learned her 20-year-old daughter, Renée, had been killed by a drunk driver. It rang five months later, and she found out her husband's 17-year-old daughter from an earlier marriage bad been killed by a drunk driver.

The phone rang in April of 1991, and Linda heard the worst again: Her remaining daughter, Leslie, 21, had been hit and killed by a drunk driver.

"I just began to beat my fist on the counter," Hull says. She remembers saying, "This can't be happening. This can't be happening to me again."

Linda and Warren Hulls only living child, Richard, is 18 and a freshman at Louisiana State University. "I would like to chain him," Hull, 51, says with a short laugh. "If it could happen to you three times, why couldn't it happen to you four times? That was one thing I had to work on. I had to try to give him space so he could grow to be his own person."

Hull credits Richard, 13 at the time of his last sister's death, with helping her turn her life around after so much violent loss. Numb from grieving, she was undergoing professional counseling. "Richard said to me one day, 'Mama, I want you to come back.' And I said, 'Come back? I haven't gone anywhere.' And be said, 'Well, I used to have a mama who talked to me, but now I don't.'

"I knew I needed to find a way to do something," Hull recalls, "because I was very depressed and had a lot of anger. I realized that I can't make these girls come back. The only thing I can do is make a change."

Less than a year after Leslie's death, Hull participated in a Mothers Against Drunk Driving tour of major cities in Louisiana, lobbying for changes in state driving-while-intoxicated (DWI) laws. She has been a key lobbyist for MADD in Louisiana ever since, a job that is not without its frustrations. For one thing, the state's liquor lobby fights hard against efforts to discourage drinking. The very culture of the state works against anti-drunk-driving efforts as well. "We're known as the party state, and we do live up to that reputation quite well, I think," Hull says. "There are hardly any activities or outings that take place without alcohol."

Since two of Hull's girls were killed by underage drinkers, she has taken a special interest in youth programs. She serves as the state coordinator for TeamSpirit, a MADD-sponsored program of the National Highway Transportation Safety Administration that trains high school students to encourage their peers to be alcohol- and drug-free. She was also instrumental in helping the Louisiana Coalition to Prevent Underage Drinking get an $839,000 grant from the Robert Wood Johnson Foundation in 1997. And she speaks often at junior high schools, high schools, and colleges. "You can't ever stop," she says. "To reach kids, the message has to be constant."

There's still much to do in Louisiana, Hull says. "As long as I hold up, I will probably do this.

"You hear a lot of people say, 'If I could change just one person. . . .'

I'm so greedy, I want to change more than one. I realize I can't change them all. But I'll always want more than one."

A Native American Message

Eulynda Toledo-Benalli believes she is alive today because her father guided her sprit back to the living world. As she lay trapped in a van, critically injured in a June 10, 1993, drunk-driving crash, her father, who had died three years earlier, appeared to her. "I remember running after him," Toledo-Benalli says. "He was checking on me, and I was saying, 'Wait for me!' And he held his hand up and said no. And left."

Now every June 10, Toledo-Benalli, 43, celebrates life, participating with her family—husband David, daughters Coral, 17, and Rainy, 6, and son, David Ross, 5—in ceremonies inspired by her Navajo tribe. "I want people to know that we need to celebrate life and appreciate it," she says.

A director of a school wilderness program, she was driving five students in a van when they were hit head-on by a drunk driver. The drunk driver died; none of the students was critically injured. Toledo-Benalli suffered a lacerated liver, two collapsed lungs and a crushed pelvis and leg. She stayed in the hospital for months, undergoing 12 surgeries and grueling physical therapy. Today Toledo-Benalli, a former mountain runner and marathoner, must walk with a cane and battles chronic pain from her injuries. Her former career in special education is too physically challenging now. "My physical self is not there anymore like I knew it," she says. "A big part of me was lost. I had to dig deep inside and find out who else I am."

Toledo-Benalli had her first contact with MADD while she was still in the hospital. As soon as she was able, she attended the Bernalillo County Victim Impact Panel, at which offenders hear how their behavior affects victims. "The first time I went, my head was hurting. I was angry, I was sad. These people represented something that had hurt me and my family very badly." She has continued to go to the panels nonetheless. When the offenders are Native Americans, Toledo-Benalli feels she has a special message for them. "I introduce myself in my language, Navajo, to let them know I'm just like them, and then I tell my story—about the crash, about my father. Because of that experience, I know that we don't take anything with us. All we take is our spirits, and how responsible we are here on earth. And that's my biggest message."

Toledo-Benalli also speaks at high schools and substance-abuse centers and to leadership groups and Native American groups. She is studying for her Ph.D. in educational psychology, focusing on Navajo women. "They have historically had a very important place in Navajo society," she says, "but that has been changed by Western thinking." She hopes her work can restore Navajo traditions that have been lost. "I'm planting seeds, you know," she says.

Losing a Daughter

On the day after her 15-year-old daughter was killed by a drunk driver, Mary Aller, a single mother, took all photographs of Karen off the walls and put them on her coffee table.

"All I could say was, 'What am I going to do now? What am I going to do?' Everything I did, I did for Karen. I didn't think I could live without her. I didn't want to live anymore."

Aller's best friend, Barbara Spuehler, knew what she was thinking. "If you do something like that," Spuehler warned, "You're not going to go to heaven."

"And that's what stopped me," Aller, 37, a U.S. Postal Service supervisor, remembers. "I hadn't been a churchgoing person, but after the crash I needed to be in church, to be close to God, because that made me feel I was close to Karen."

Spuehler also contacted MADD, which put Aller in touch with a support group. Karen was killed in October 1991; four months later, Aller, still grieving, began to work actively with MADD. She and Spuehler founded the Westchester County chapter in 1992. Today it has 125 members and Aller is serving her first term as chapter president

"I'll do whatever the chapter asks me to do," Aller says. Through the years, that has included participating in victims' vigils and even dressing up as the Lion King for a parade. A special passion is lobbying for stronger drunk-driving penalties in New York. The driver who killed Karen as she walked the few blocks home from her high school fled the scene and was arrested on the day of Karen's burial; he spent only a few months in jail.

Aller helped establish Westchester County's Victim Impact Panel. "I hate going to those things," Aller says, "but I know it's something I have to do to keep Karen's memory alive. And if I get through to one person in that room, it's worth the effort."

True to Karen's memory, Aller believes her most important work is with young people. She speaks in schools or at youth gatherings anytime she's asked. Aller often cries as she tells her story. "I just want these kids to know that they're not invincible," she says. "It can happen to them. I tell them to think about their parents. Would they want their mother and father to go through what I'm going through?

"I miss my daughter every day," Aller says, "but I feel like I've come a long way. We were best friends. And now, when I have a dilemma about something, I ask myself, 'What would Karen want me to do?'"

A Traumatized Family

The Valone family survived the horrible night of February 9, 1990, but it greatly changed them.

Hit head-on by a drunk driver, all four Valones suffered critical injuries. Husband Don received trauma to the brain and broken legs and ribs. Seven years later, he has attention deficit disorder and problems with his memory. Samantha, age 9 at the time of the crash, suffered internal injuries, fractured vertebrae, and a head injury that has left her with lasting difficulty in reading and comprehension.

Kathleen Valone's legs were broken, her knees crushed, her heart and lungs bruised. Despite these injuries, she managed to stagger to one of the ambulances on the scene to be with her youngest daughter, Jamie, 7, as she was rushed to the hospital with a severe brain injury and a tear in the brain lining. At the emergency room, mother and daughter were separated. Valone could hear doctors call a Code Blue and shouted across the emergency room, "Jamie, Mom loves you." Remembering today, she cries softly. "I like to think that helped pull her through."

Jamie, now 15, did survive, but the accident left her with severe learning disabilities and epilepsy. She needs close supervision, provided mostly by her mother. Kathleen Valone herself, at 42, walks with a cane and will need to have her knees replaced at some point.

Despite their personal challenges, Kathleen and Don Valone have become two of MADD's most valuable players in the state of Michigan. Don Valone, who works at Kmart's national headquarters in Troy, is state chairman of MADD Michigan. Kathleen Valone is active in MADD chapters in Oakland County, where the Valones used to live, and in Lapeer County, where they now live. She often speaks to youth groups and at junior high schools and high schools, and has become a supporter and role model for other parents whose children have suffered impairment as a result of drunk driving.

"There's one reason that drives me to do everything I'm doing," she says. "In order for me to live with what's happened to us and to get through each day, I have to make something good out of something bad."

She has plenty of experience doing that. When the public schools didn't have a program suitable for Jamie's disability, the Valones, along with other parents, started a private school, North Star Academy, specifically for learning-disabled children. In 1997, North Star Academy had 25 students and five teachers. And though it's located 55 miles from where the Valones live, Kathleen makes sure Jamie gets there every day.

"There was a time when we had more bad days than good," Valone says. "We have more good days than bad now."

Talking to Survivors

Stephanie Denham, 39, doesn't allow herself to imagine the future very much. "Part of my future was taken away from me," Denham says, "so I no longer assume that things are going to happen the way I want them to."

The event that changed Denham's life forever occurred on Palm Sunday in 1991, shortly after her family had returned from church.

Denham's oldest daughter, Lorien, then 9, had a soccer game that afternoon, and at the last minute, Stephanie and younger daughter Sarah decided not to go. Denham's husband, David, and Lorien were on their way to the game when they were struck by a drunk driver who was speeding through a red light. The crash seriously injured David Denham; to this day he has trouble walking and suffers some memory loss.

Lorien was dealt massive injuries. She suffered a shattered skull, brain injuries, and broken bones in her face, elbows, hip, and pelvis. When Stephanie Denham got to the hospital, an emergency room nurse told her, "You can see your husband, but we're still working on your daughter."

"I knew what that meant," remembers Denham, herself a registered nurse. Lorien was taken to surgery, but there wasn't much that could be done. Five days after the crash, she died. Her remaining healthy organs were donated, a decision Lorien had made herself just a year before after seeing her mother mark her driver's license for organ donation.

Within two weeks of Lorien's burial, Denham gave a speech encouraging organ donation. Within a month, a group approached the Denhams about forming a MADD chapter in their county. They did; the chapter was named after Lorien.

Denham got deeply involved in MADD: speaking at Victim Impact Panels, counseling victims, and lobbying for tougher DWI laws in Mississippi. In 1994, the state organization, MADD Mississippi, was in disarray; Denham stepped in to help revive it and is now serving in her third and final year as state board chairwoman.

It's an impressive slate of activities, particularly in light of the fact that Denham is a working wife and mother who is also active in her church. "The basic thing that motivates me is that I don't want another family to go through what we've gone through," she says. "I keep going because I think, What if I don't reach the person I'm supposed to do something about?"

Meanwhile, the man who killed Lorien remains in a Mississippi prison, serving 30 years without parole. "He got the stiffest sentence ever handed down in Mississippi for a single DWI death," says Denham. "We got justice. I have found when I speak to groups of DWI survivors and victims that our story gives them encouragement and hope that justice can be done."

THE FRIEND I WOULD HAVE LEAST SUSPECTED

Randy Wayne White

In the following selection, journalist Randy Wayne White describes his efforts to understand why a friend who seldom drank would be arrested for driving under the influence (DUI). According to White, his friend was stopped at a DUI checkpoint on the way home from a wedding where he had had a small amount to drink. Although White's friend was convinced that he was not drunk, his Breathalyzer test registered the state's minimum for intoxication (.08 percent), and he was arrested. Amazed at the consequences of his friend's mistake, White decided to do his own research on drunk driving, accompanying DUI patrol officers on their rounds and taking a roadside sobriety test. Even though White had not been drinking when he took the test, he writes that the experience was humiliating. However, the real problems begin after the arrest, White explains, when drunk drivers pay for their mistakes in fines, legal fees, revoked licenses, and lost jobs. Worst of all, he concludes, some must live with the fact that they have taken a human life.

Middle age is what military experts might describe as a "target-rich environment." Your simplest mistakes can gather horrible momentum and velocity, like the arc of electricity or the flow of water. I watched the process from close range when a friend called and said, "You're not going to believe who just got arrested for DUI [driving under the influence]." He was right. Out of all my many hard-living, coconut-headed friends, the man he named was the one I would have least suspected. I've known him for a dozen years. He's a superb athlete and a successful businessman. I telephoned him to find out what had happened.

A Painful Lesson

"It's so ridiculous, I still can't believe it," he told me. "My friend's daughter got married and I went to the wedding. I don't particularly like alcohol and I almost never have more than a drink or two

Reprinted, by permission of the author, from "Ten Steps to Screw Up Your Life," by Randy Wayne White, *Men's Health*, April 1999.

because I hate the way it makes me feel."

It was true that in all the years I'd known him, this guy had never participated in the beery excesses so beloved of my other friends and me.

"But it was a wedding, right? There were toasts, and I had one glass of wine. One, that's all. The reception had kind of a Jimmy Buffett theme, so the father of the bride made his special margaritas. I didn't even finish mine because it was so strong. Then there was a final toast, a glass of champagne. That's all I had, period."

My friend had a short drive home. It was early on a Sunday evening. Near the entrance to his subdivision, the local sheriff's department had set up a DUI checkpoint.

"I stepped out of the car and chatted with the deputies while they administered roadside breathalyzers. They were only testing every third driver, but I was curious about the test. When they asked, I told them honestly where I'd been and how much I'd had to drink. I voluntarily took the breathalyzer. I didn't feel the least bit drunk, so what did I have to fear?"

What did he have to fear? The same thing we should all fear. Here's the revelation: Stupidity destroys more guys like us than heart attacks do. Death, at least, is an attention-getter. Stupidity provides its own cover. There are a thousand creative ways to screw up our lives, yet most of us tumble into the same idiotic traps, generation after generation.

Still, my friend was setting a new standard for dumb. In a lot of states, refusing the test is the same as flunking it. But *asking* for it? That's really asking for it.

"You told a cop you'd been drinking, then volunteered to take a breathalyzer?" I said to my friend. "Jeez! What a moron! You deserved to be arrested just for being so dumb."

"But I wasn't being dumb, I was being cooperative. And honest!"

Okay, he was a cooperative, honest, dumb guy. By the time we reach middle age, it's endemic. Why? Maybe it's because as we age, our network of family and hangers-on expands exponentially, as do our economic, business, and civic obligations. Metaphorically, we are bigger people. We are also easier targets. Unfortunately, neither our intellect nor our perspective grows proportionately. To prove it, I polled more than 300 good men, asking what had screwed up their lives. The responses were touchingly similar. Near the top of the list, along with mistresses and custody battles, was getting arrested for driving under the influence.

Conducting Personal Research

There is only one way to research such behavior effectively. I had to write about it from the inside. To that end, I arranged to ride around with DUI patrol officers from various law-enforcement agencies in my home state. And just to show my dumb friend that he wasn't alone, I, too, offered to take a roadside sobriety test.

"I have guys your age break down and cry when I pull them over," one deputy told me. "They tell me a DUI will cost them their jobs, maybe even their professions. But know what? I'm not the one who poured booze down their throats and put car keys in their hands. I've got a job to do and I do it."

This deputy's no-nonsense attitude added a discomforting realism when he administered the field sobriety test. Even though I hadn't had any alcohol for more than two weeks, it was scary and demeaning as hell. I felt like potential roadkill, standing in the parking lot of a cheap motel, performing inane, Simon-says acrobatics.

First he had me follow a moving penlight, eyes only: the horizontal-gaze nystagmus test. This seemed like an innocuous little exercise, but it was actually the most telling, he said. If you've been drinking, your eyeballs jerk reflexively at a certain angle of deviation. "No way you can fake it," the deputy told me. "Once I see your eyes, I know if you have a significant amount of alcohol in your system."

Next, I took the walk-the-line test, heel to toe, which I goofed up. "You're not listening to the directions," he said. "It's one of the things we look for. Drunks don't listen and they can't remember what they hear."

If I'd had a beer or two in my system and keys in my hand, the officer might have cuffed me and driven me to the county jail for a breathalyzer. Frightening? You bet.

It turns a lot scarier once they put you behind bars. Just ask my nice, athletic friend. His breathalyzer registered his state's minimum standard for intoxication: 0.08.

"I smiled when the cop told me," my friend said. "Even he agreed that I didn't seem the least bit intoxicated."

It didn't matter. My friend was handcuffed, read his Miranda rights, and put into the back of a police cruiser. From there he was taken to the county jail, where he was searched, allowed one phone call, and locked in a cell with 10 other prisoners and one seatless toilet in the corner.

Facing the Consequences

"It was surreal," my friend said. "I wasn't drunk, I wasn't a criminal, but there I was locked up with all these screaming, shouting jackasses. A couple of guys were puking, fighting over the toilet. Another guy was barking like a crazed dog. I stayed in there for nearly 10 hours, not knowing what the hell was going on. What were my wife and kids thinking?"

It gets weirder. Twenty-five years earlier, after a fraternity party, my friend had been arrested for drunk driving. "It was largely because of that experience that I've always avoided excessive drinking. It didn't matter. It was my second offense. Even though, as a driver, I've never had a moving violation, never been in an accident, never had any other kind of trouble with the law, I was screwed."

My friend had to pay what he estimates to be $4,000 in court fines, DUI school fines, and attorney's fees. His car was impounded. He was sentenced to 50 hours of community service—picking up trash along the road. His driver's license was revoked for a year and, because it was his second offense, he couldn't get a hardship permit, which would at least let him drive to and from work. And if he's caught driving with a suspended license, the fines are multiplied and he'll probably do jail time.

"My attorneys are still working on my license," he told me. "Meanwhile, corporate headquarters has made it very clear that my future with them is now limited. This has damaged my life in ways that are far out of proportion to what I did. This is a cloud on my life and the lives of my family that will never go away."

Another guy I know had "a couple of drinks" at a dance club only a mile or so from his home. He then got behind the wheel of his car. In the growing darkness, he hit and killed a 16-year-old boy.

"Every morning I wake up and I wish I'd died that night," the man told me recently. That night was 7 years ago. He's still in his 40s.

"I remember feeling very good that evening. Things were going well, my business was doing great. It was dark, my attention wandered, and next thing I knew, I was pulled off along the side of the road and someone was screaming, 'He's dead! He's dead!' That quickly, the boy's life was over. So was mine."

A lightning strike? Not really. According to data compiled by the National Highway Traffic Safety Administration, 16,189 people were killed in crashes involving alcohol in 1997. Do the math: That's 311 people a week, the equivalent of one jumbo-jet crash every 7 days.

"I've tried to rebuild my life," the man told me. "As a public service, I agreed to speak to a high-school driver's-ed class, to tell them how idiotic it is to risk taking a drink and then get behind the wheel. The first class I spoke to, I looked into the faces of those kids and I saw that they despised me. It turned out that the boy I killed had been a classmate of theirs. They made me leave, and I don't blame them."

Neither do I. Neither does my friend. He lucked out. He only went to jail.

LEARNING THE HARD WAY

Michael Denne

In the following article, written while serving time at Folsom State Prison in Sacramento, California, for his hit-and-run drunk driving conviction, Michael Denne states that he accepts responsibility for the damage done to two teenagers who were seriously injured in an accident he caused while driving under the influence of alcohol. Denne maintains, however, that the victims are not the only ones who suffer in drunk driving accidents: Perpetrators also pay a great price for their crime. For instance, Denne reveals that due to his actions, he lost his driver's license, his car, a good job, and his freedom. In addition, he must bear the emotional weight of the pain he has inflicted on others. Although he is ashamed of his behavior, Denne writes that he wants to let people know about his crime so that his example can serve as a warning to others who might be tempted to drink and drive.

It was after midnight when the police came for me. I was standing in the kitchen, stunned, not sure what had just happened or what to do about it. But it all became surrealistically clear as I was led from my own house in handcuffs, bathed in flashing colored lights. Having gone only a few hundred yards on our way to the station, we came upon more flashing lights at the scene of an accident. "See that," the cop snapped at me. "You did that."

It's not easy being a menace to society, especially when you always thought you were one of the good guys. But that same society takes a particularly dim view of those of us who drink to excess, crash our cars and send innocent people to the emergency room with life-threatening injuries. So dim a view, in fact, that they send us to prison.

Before you despise me too much, though, I'd like to report that no one was crippled or killed as a result of my selfish stupidity. Two teenagers did, however, spend a few weeks in the hospital and several months recovering, as they both suffered head trauma from my Chevy Blazer's broadsiding their Mazda RX-7. Nine months after the crash, at my sentencing hearing, the victims appeared as two walking, talking, healthy-looking young adults. Their injuries lingered, though, in the form of a loss of hearing in one ear (for the girl), which may or may not come back, and memory loss (for the boy, who also broke his jaw and was semicomatose for a few weeks). Not quite as good as new, but awfully close and improving, considering their condition that first night in intensive care.

I offer no excuse because there isn't one. What I did was the height of irresponsibility. Like everyone else, I've seen hit-and-run accidents on television and in the newspapers and wondered how the drivers could leave the victims behind. Well, I did, and I still don't know. It's called hit and run, but I didn't run anywhere. I wasn't wearing a seat belt and I'd slammed my head into the windshield. I was shocked, and so close to home I thought that if I could just get to that sanctuary, I'd know what to do and everything would be all right. But somewhere in my beer-soaked brain must have been the fear that generated more concern for myself than for anyone I might have hurt. And I have to live with that.

I've been locked up for more than a year now and have had plenty of time to think. It seems to me that there's a price exacted for every lesson we learn in life, and the cost is rarely proportional to the relative simplicity or complexity of the idea. Consequently, what should have been a no-brainer is quite often the most expensive education we're ever likely to receive. What it cost me to ignore the most ubiquitous warning in the world (the one not to drink and drive) was merely everything: my license, my car, $30,000 in legal fees, a $50,000-a-year job I'd had for 10 years and my freedom are all casualties—with my house not far behind.

For far too many people this subject will forever be anathema, because the lives of their loved ones have been ruined or ended by some recreational inebriate just like me. To them and countless others I got exactly what I deserve, even though an excellent recovery and $530,000 of liability insurance appear to have left the victims in pretty good shape. I'll not portray myself as some drunken Robin Hood, because these people truly suffered, but they are not from wealthy families and now may well have opportunities they otherwise would never have had. And that's good; they deserve it.

I refuse to vilify the "demon" alcohol, because that's not what this is about. It's about responsibility. A few years ago, Miller Brewing Co. promoted an awareness campaign with the slogan "Think when you drink." That's good, but it doesn't go far enough, because we can't think when we drink. It's got to be "Think before you drink"—because as any substance-abuse professional will tell you, judgment is the first faculty that goes.

In his book of essays "Fates Worse Than Death," Kurt Vonnegut wrote, "Life without moments of intoxication is not worth a pitcher of spit." Included therein is intoxication from love or joy or the mystery of life itself, but so is, surely, a few belts at the corner bar. I'm no social scientist, but like anyone who's ever taken a college anthropology class, I learned that the society without a way to alter its perception is the exception to the rule. It is not aberrant behavior to celebrate, to alter one's consciousness, and to think that people will or should stop it is naive. But when it has a profoundly negative impact on the lives of others, it is totally unacceptable. In fact, it can be downright criminal.

My negligence was exactly that, though I am innocent of malice, of intent ever to hurt anyone. But it doesn't matter what you mean to do—it matters what you do. And few people know that better than I do.

The probation report said I'd led a respectable life but I should get six years in prison, anyway. The district attorney said I was a decent man and he felt sorry for me, but six years wasn't enough—I should do eight instead. And the judge agreed, but in his benevolence ruled that the extra two years could be served concurrently. There isn't space here to debate the deterrent value of a state prison sentence as opposed to alternative sentences, like making restitution to the injured through a work-furlough program or explaining the consequences of drinking and driving to high-school students, punishments that contain real value for the victims and the community.

That I deserve to be punished is clearer to me than it ever could be to anyone who hasn't lived it. Until you wake up in a jail cell, not knowing whether the people now in the hospital will be permanently disfigured (or will cease to be altogether) as a result of your recklessness, you can't imagine how it feels. The weight of it is oppressive.

I'm ashamed to have to lend my name to some of the most loathsome behavior known, but not so much so that I won't put forth a face and a fair warning to those who still choose to drink and drive: thinking it could never happen to you is your first mistake—and it only gets worse from there. For everyone.

CHAPTER 3

SOLUTIONS TO THE PROBLEM OF DRUNK DRIVING

PREVENTING DRUNK DRIVING: AN OVERVIEW

Ralph Hingson

In the following article, Ralph Hingson reviews some of the efforts that states have taken to prevent drunk driving. He examines different types of legislation, which he divides into the categories of general and specific deterrence laws. General deterrence laws, Hingson explains, are intended to prevent drivers from ever driving drunk; they include laws that make it a criminal offense to drive with a blood alcohol concentration (BAC) above a certain limit. Specific deterrence laws are penalties applied to those who are arrested for drunk driving more than once, he writes, and include jail sentences, treatment programs, and license-plate impoundment. The author believes that in addition to these laws, rigorous enforcement, community intervention, grass roots activism, and public education can have an impact in reducing drunk driving. Hingson is the chair of the social and behavioral sciences department at the Boston University School of Public Health in Massachusetts.

Even at blood alcohol concentrations (BAC's) as low as 0.02 percent, alcohol affects driver performance by reducing reaction time and slowing the decision-making process. Epidemiological research comparing BAC's of drivers in single-vehicle fatal crashes with those of drivers stopped at random in nationwide surveys indicates that each 0.02-percent increase in BAC nearly doubles a driver's risk of being in a fatal crash. The risk increases more rapidly with each drink for drivers under age 21, who have less experience in driving and who, as a group, more often take risks in traffic, such as speeding or failing to wear seatbelts. For all groups of drivers, fatal crash involvement per miles driven increases ninefold at BAC's of 0.05 to 0.09 percent.

In 1995 there were 17,274 alcohol-related traffic fatalities and approximately 300,000 persons injured in alcohol-related crashes. Young people, people previously convicted for driving under the influence (DUI), and males in general are disproportionately involved

Excerpted from "Prevention of Drinking and Driving," by Ralph Hingson, *Alcohol Health and Research World*, vol. 20, no. 4 (1996), a publication of the U.S. government. References in the original have been omitted here but are available from the author.

in alcohol-related traffic deaths. Approximately three in five Americans will be involved in an alcohol-related crash at some point in their lives. In addition, alcohol-impaired driving often has an impact on innocent victims. In 1995, 39 percent of people killed in crashes involving drivers who had been drinking were persons other than the drinking driver.

Alcohol-related traffic crashes cost society $45 billion annually in hospital costs, rehabilitation expenses, and lost productivity. In 1995 more than 1.4 million people were arrested for driving while intoxicated, nearly 10 percent of all arrests made that year.

Alcohol-Related Traffic Deaths

The United States, like several other countries, has experienced marked declines in recent years in the number of fatal crashes involving alcohol. In 1982, when the National Highway Traffic Safety Administration (NHTSA) began estimating the proportion of fatal crashes nationwide that involved alcohol, 25,165 fatal crashes (57.2 percent of all fatal crashes) involved a driver or pedestrian who had been drinking. In 1995 alcohol was involved in 17,274 crash fatalities, or 41.3 percent of all crash fatalities. Between 1982 and 1995, the proportion of crash fatalities involving alcohol fell by 28 percent, and the number of crash fatalities involving alcohol dropped by 31 percent.

Many improvements in traffic safety have occurred since 1982, such as the adoption of laws requiring the use of child restraints in all States and the enactment of legislation mandating the use of seatbelts in 49 States. However, the decline in alcohol-related traffic deaths was independent of these laws: Traffic deaths that did not involve alcohol increased 28 percent from 18,780 in 1982 to 24,524 in 1995.

The greatest declines in alcohol-related traffic deaths were among youth under 21. Among people ages 15 to 20, alcohol-related traffic deaths declined by 59 percent between 1982 and 1995, from 5,380 to 2,201. In this age group, the proportion of fatalities involving alcohol declined from 63 percent in 1982 to 36 percent in 1995, a 43-percent decline. Despite the long-term decline since 1982 in alcohol-related traffic deaths, a 4-percent increase in such deaths (from 16,589 to 17,274) occurred between 1994 and 1995, the first increase in 10 years. The increase occurred among persons age 21 and over.

Reducing Drunk Driving

A key social change behind efforts to reduce drunk driving was the establishment in the early 1980's of grass roots organizations such as Mothers Against Drunk Driving (MADD), Students Against Drunk Driving (SADD), and Remove Intoxicated Drivers (RID). Along with its support for victims affected by drunk drivers and its public education activities, MADD monitors research findings and, through legislative compendia, workshops, and national report cards rating the States, presents findings from this research and other testimony to State legislators. According to NHTSA, since 1982 more than 2,000 State laws have been passed in an effort to reduce alcohol-impaired driving. MADD has been an important force behind many of those laws.

Several factors make it difficult for researchers to isolate the effects of specific laws in reducing drunk driving. First, several laws are often passed in a given State within a relatively short time period, making it difficult to separate fully the effects of each law. Second, publicity about the drunk-driving problem is aired across State borders, diminishing any differences that may be found between States with different legislation.

Third, because most States do not determine BAC's of all drivers involved in fatal crashes, researchers often rely on surrogate (i.e., proxy) measures of alcohol involvement in fatal crashes, such as single-vehicle nighttime (SVN) fatal crashes. SVN fatal crashes are three times more likely than other fatal crashes to involve alcohol. However, this proxy measure can be conservative: SVN fatal crashes account for less than one-half of all fatal traffic crashes involving intoxicated drivers. Consequently, the use of surrogate measures introduces some imprecision in evaluating the effects of legislation, particularly in short-term studies involving small jurisdictions. Variability in outcome measures from study to study makes cross-study comparisons difficult.

Fourth, people who drive after heavy drinking (defined as five or more drinks at one sitting) are much more likely to engage in other risky driving behaviors, such as speeding, running red lights, making illegal turns, driving after other drug use, and failing to wear seatbelts. Therefore, studies should control for shifts in legislation, targeting these behaviors (i.e., increased enforcement of traffic laws) as well as measuring overall changes in these behaviors.

Despite these methodological concerns, a number of conclusions can be reached concerning the effects of various legislative interventions in reducing alcohol-impaired driving.

Legal efforts to reduce alcohol-impaired driving have emphasized deterrence. Deterrence laws seek to prevent alcohol-involved driving—through swift, certain, and severe penalties if warranted. Deterrence laws fall into two categories: (1) general deterrence laws, which aim to prevent the general public from ever driving after drinking, and (2) specific deterrence laws, which seek to prevent convicted DUI offenders from repeating their offense. Although convicted DUI offenders are at greater risk than other drivers for subsequent rearrest and crash involvement, most drivers in fatal crashes involving alcohol have never been previously convicted. In fact, two-thirds of persons arrested for DUI have never been arrested before. This statistic underscores the important need for laws and programs aimed at both general and specific deterrence.

General Deterrence Laws

As of 1996, in all States it was illegal to sell alcohol to persons under age 21. Numerous research studies indicate that raising the minimum legal drinking age (MLDA) to 21 reduces alcohol-related fatal crash involvement among youth. States adopting MLDA's of 21 in the early 1980's experienced a 10- to 15-percent decline in alcohol-related traffic deaths among drivers in the targeted ages, compared with States that did not adopt such laws. NHTSA estimated that MLDA's of 21 have prevented more than 14,800 traffic deaths since 1976, approximately 700 to 1,000 deaths annually for the past decade. MLDA laws not only have reduced drinking among persons under age 21, they also have lowered drinking among people ages 21 to 25 who grew up in States with MLDA's of 21 relative to those who grew up in other States.

Other nations that do not have an MLDA of 21 have experienced declines in alcohol-related fatalities among drivers under 21, as have many States that did not initially adopt an MLDA of 21. However, the evidence is clear and rather consistent that U.S. States which raised the legal drinking age experienced greater declines in fatal crashes likely to involve alcohol among drivers under 21 than did States that initially retained lower drinking ages.

As of 1996, every State except Massachusetts and South Carolina had adopted laws that make it a criminal offense per se to drive with a BAC above the State's legal limit, which is generally either 0.10 or 0.08 percent. The per se provision means that prosecutors do not have to introduce evidence other than BAC to demonstrate impairment, making convictions easier to obtain.

Administrative license suspension laws allow a police officer or other official to immediately confiscate the license of a driver whose BAC exceeds the legal limit. License actions thus occur closer to the time of infraction and, by bypassing the court, are more swift and certain. Although these laws have faced some challenges for allegedly imposing double jeopardy on a driver who subsequently is convicted of DUI and receives additional penalties, no State supreme court has upheld such a challenge. In 1988 the Insurance Institute for Highway Safety conducted a nationwide comparison of administrative revocation laws, criminal per se laws, mandatory jail laws, and community service laws passed between 1978 and 1985. Administrative license revocation laws were accompanied by a 5-percent decline in fatal crashes, compared with a 2-percent decline for other types of laws, such as criminal per se laws.

By 1996, 37 States and the District of Columbia had adopted zero-tolerance legislation, laws that make it illegal for drivers under 21 to drive after drinking any alcohol. Laws setting legal BAC limits of 0.00 to 0.02 percent are considered zero-tolerance laws. A recent study compared the first 12 States that lowered legal BAC's for drivers under 21 with 12 nearby States that did not. States adopting zero-tolerance laws experienced a 20-percent greater decline in the proportion of SVN fatal crashes among 15- to 20-year-old drivers. States lowering BAC limits to 0.04 or 0.06 did not experience significant declines relative to comparison States in the proportion of SVN fatal crashes among this age group. The study projected that if the remaining States adopted zero-tolerance laws and experienced comparable declines, 375 to 400 fewer fatal crashes would occur each year. Zero-tolerance laws may be effective because they convey a clear message to youth: Drivers under 21 may not drive after any alcohol consumption whatsoever.

One problem encountered in implementing these laws has been the difficulty in achieving broad awareness of the law. Studies in California and Massachusetts found that 45 to 50 percent of young drivers were unaware of the law. R. Blomberg, in a quasi-experimental study of an awareness campaign involving public service announcements about Maryland's zero-tolerance law, found a one-third greater decline in alcohol-involved crashes among drivers receiving intensive education than among drivers who received no intensive education.

Lowering the Per Se Laws

By 1996, 13 States had adopted criminal per se laws lowering the legal BAC from 0.10 to 0.08 percent. Massachusetts has set the BAC for its administrative license revocation law at 0.08 percent.

D. Johnson and M. Waitz monitored six different measures of driver alcohol involvement in the first five States to adopt 0.08-percent per se laws and identified several statistically significant pre- to post-law decreases. However, comparison areas with different per se limits were not included; the study therefore could not determine whether post-law declines were independent of general regional trends.

A subsequent analysis paired the first five States to adopt a 0.08-percent legal BAC limit with five nearby States that retained the 0.10-percent legal limit. As a group, States that adopted the 0.08-percent limit experienced a statistically significant 16-percent post-law decline in the proportion of fatal crashes involving fatally injured drivers at 0.08-percent BAC and higher. They also experienced a statistically significant 18-percent post-law decline in the proportion of fatal crashes involving fatally injured drivers at 0.15-percent BAC and higher. Four of the five 0.08-percent States experienced greater post-law declines than did comparison States. In the three largest of the five 0.08-percent States, the declines were significantly greater than in their respective comparison States. Those three pairs of States accounted for more than 90 percent of the fatal crashes in the study. During the pre- and post-law period, more than 80 percent of fatally injured drivers were given blood alcohol tests in 0.08-percent States.

Compared with 0.10-percent States, the 0.08-percent States may have been more concerned about alcohol-impaired driving and more responsive to legislative initiatives to reduce the problem. All five 0.08-percent States had administrative license revocation laws during the study period, three of which were implemented within one year of the 0.08-percent law. Administrative license revocation laws have been associated with a 5-percent decline in fatal crashes and as much as a 9-percent decline in alcohol-related fatal crashes. This potential effect restricted the study's ability to separate the effect of 0.08-percent laws from that of administrative license revocation laws. Only in Maine was administrative license revocation in place throughout the pre-law analysis period prior to adoption of the reduced BAC limit. Thus, Maine was the only State where it was possible to identify an independent effect of the 0.08-percent law.

The results of this study suggest that 0.08-percent laws combined with administrative license revocation can reduce the proportion both of fatal crashes involving drivers and of fatally injured drivers at 0.08-percent BAC or higher and at 0.15-percent BAC or higher. The study projected that if all States adopted 0.08-percent laws—with results similar to those of the first five States to adopt such laws—at least 500 to 600 fewer deaths would occur on the Nation's roadways each year.

In 1994 Massachusetts simultaneously introduced a 0.08-percent BAC and administrative license revocation laws. Statewide randomized telephone surveys in 1993 (i.e., before the 0.08-percent BAC law was implemented) and in 1996 (i.e., after the law was implemented) revealed clear shifts in public perceptions of how much drivers could drink and still drive safely and legally. The proportion of respondents who believed they could consume four or more drinks and drive safely declined from 24 to 15 percent, and the proportion who felt they could drive legally after more than four drinks dropped from 18 to 9 percent. At the same time, the proportion of respondents who believed drunk drivers would have their license suspended before a trial rose from 47 to 71 percent. In addition, the proportion of drivers who reported driving in the past month after consuming four or more drinks declined from 9 to 4 percent.

Specific Deterrence Laws

Persons convicted of alcohol-impaired driving are more likely than other drivers to be subsequently arrested for driving while intoxicated and to be involved in alcohol-related crashes. Specific deterrence laws seek to reduce this recidivism through license actions, treatment or rehabilitation, jail sentences, dedicated detention, probation, actions against vehicles and vehicle tags, lower legal BAC's for offenders, or some combination of these measures.

Mandatory license suspensions are more effective than discretionary suspension in reducing total crashes and violations. Their effectiveness is attributed to the fact that the laws generate a perceived certainty of punishment and reduce the influence of judicial discretion. Evidence also indicates that diversion to treatment with either a restricted or a limited license leads to higher accident and violation rates than full license suspension. Several studies also report that full license suspension reduces DUI recidivism. Much of this benefit may result from reduced driving exposure.

NHTSA and the National Institute on Alcohol Abuse and Alcoholism (NIAAA) prepared *A Guide to Sentencing DUI Offenders* and reported the following:

- Suspension periods between 12 and 18 months appear to be optimal for reducing DUI recidivism.
- Suspension periods of less than three months seem to be ineffective.
- Although more than 50 percent of persons with suspended licenses continue to drive, they seem to drive less frequently and more cautiously in order to avoid arrest.

In 1995, E. Wells-Parker, R. Bangert Drowns, R. McMillan, and M. Williams completed a meta-analysis of treatment efficacy for DUI offenders. Compared with standard sanctions (i.e., jail or fines) or no treatment, rehabilitation generated a 7- to 9-percent reduction in the incidence of alcohol-related driving recidivism and crashes when averaged across all types of offenders and rehabilitation. Alcohol-related crashes and violations constitute only a minority of total crashes and violations. Actions to restrict license use (e.g., daytime-only driving permits) combined with some kind of remedial treatment have been found to be more effective in preventing alcohol-related traffic incidents than full suspension.

The analysis by Wells-Parker and colleagues also indicated that treatments combining punishment strategies, education, and therapy with follow-up monitoring and aftercare were more effective for first-time as well as repeat offenders than any single approach. For example, combining treatment with licensing action was more effective than either tactic alone. According to this analysis, treatment alone never substitutes for sanctions or remedies, and remedies and sanctions do not substitute for treatment. Finally, weekend intervention programs designed to evaluate alcohol and other drug abuse and create an individualized treatment plan for offenders have been found to produce lower recidivism rates than jail, suspended sentences, or fines.

Incarceration and Detention

Although incarceration incapacitates drivers during the period of confinement, minimal evidence exists on the postincarceration effect of jail. Nichols and Ross (reviewed in the NHTSA and NIAAA sentencing guide) examined the specific deterrent effects of jail sentences for first-time and repeat DUI offenders in a review of more than 80 studies of legal deterrence. Eight studies reported no reductions in DUI recidivism as a result of jail sentences, and only one recent study provided reasonably convincing evidence of a three-year reduction for first-time repeat offenders who received mandatory two-day jail sentences in Tennessee. In one study, long periods of incarceration were actually associated with higher recidivism. Although jail sentences may have some short-term general deterrent effects, as well as deterrent effects for first-time offenders, mandatory jail sentences tend to affect court operations and the correctional process negatively by increasing the demand for jury trials and plea bargains and by crowding jails.

Detention facilities specifically for DUI offenders can offer both incapacitation and supervised rehabilitation services. One program of this type, in Prince Georges County, Maryland, has been found to reduce recidivism among both first-time and repeat offenders.

The 1996 NHTSA-NIAAA review of sentencing options found that probation may slightly reduce recidivism among drivers at low risk for being repeat offenders, but probation alone does not measurably reduce recidivism among those at high risk. Although the effects of intensive probation and home detention have not been evaluated, a seven-year study of electronic monitoring found that recidivism rates were less than 3 percent for a group of DUI offenders who were electronically monitored during 203 months of their combined probation. However, recidivism increased when the monitoring ended.

Actions Against Vehicles and Tags

Although license actions have been shown to reduce recidivism, many people with suspended licenses continue to drive.

Unlicensed drivers can be apprehended only when police have probable cause to stop their vehicle. Washington and Oregon have enacted legislation that allows police to seize the vehicle registration of drivers caught driving after suspension, leaving the motorist with a temporary, 60-day registration. A sticker on the vehicle gives the police probable cause to stop the vehicle to ask for proof of license. Researchers have reported evidence of the law's effectiveness in Oregon but not in Washington.

A. Rodgers measured the effectiveness of the 1988 license-plate impoundment law for one-third of the DUI offenders in Minnesota. During the 29 months that the courts administered the system, only 6 percent of 7,698 eligible third-time offenders had their license plates impounded. During the 21 months in which the law was managed through the Department of Public Safety, 68 percent of the 4,593 third-time DUI offenders had vehicle plates impounded. The law had little deterrent effect while the courts administered the system. In contrast, when the program was managed administratively, offenders who lost their plates had a lower rate of recidivism than those who did not.

Another approach—ignition interlocks to prevent vehicle operation when a driver's breath alcohol exceeds a designated limit—has been found to reduce recidivism, but recidivism may rise after the device is removed.

The NHTSA-NIAAA sentencing guide identified several other sentencing approaches that have not been systematically evaluated, including financial sanctions, publication of offenders' names in newspapers, attendance at victim-impact panels, victim-restitution programs, and court-ordered visits to emergency rooms.

Despite the fact that persons convicted of DUI are more likely than other drivers to be subsequently arrested for DUI or to be involved in crashes, almost all States allow the same legal BAC for these drivers as for drivers who have never been convicted of DUI. One exception is Maine. In 1988 the State set the legal limit at 0.04 percent for drivers previously convicted for DUI, lower than the 0.08 percent limit for other drivers. In the three years following enactment of the law, nighttime fatal crashes involving drivers with prior convictions declined by 38 percent, whereas such crashes increased by 50 percent in neighboring New Hampshire and Vermont.

Enforcement of Impaired Driving Laws

The extent to which drunk-driving laws are enforced can influence their impact on impaired driving. Drunk-driving arrests increased dramatically between 1978 and 1983, from 1.3 to 1.9 million, but arrests have dropped each year since then, to 1.4 million in 1994. Estimates indicate that only one arrest is made for every 300 to 1,000 drunk-driving trips. Respondents in a 1995 national survey of 4,000 randomly selected drivers believed that people who drink and drive are more likely to be in an accident than to be stopped by the police. Only 23 percent of the respondents thought it very likely that people who drive after drinking will be stopped by the police, down from 26 percent in 1993.

The most dramatic example of the potential deterrent impact of police enforcement of drunk-driving laws occurred in Australia in New South Wales and Victoria, where random breath testing was introduced on a massive scale. In a given year, as many as one driver in three was stopped by the police. There was an immediate 37-percent drop in alcohol-related fatal crashes, compared with the previous three years, and a sustained 24-percent decrease over the next five years.

In the United States, police do not have the authority to administer breath tests to individual drivers who have been stopped unless there is probable cause to believe that the driver is under the influence of alcohol. Instead, police must use surveillance by police patrols or sobriety checkpoints, often at predesignated, high-risk areas and involving several patrol officers. Several evaluations of sobriety checkpoints have demonstrated their effectiveness. One California study found that checkpoints reduced alcohol-related crashes regardless of the way in which they were implemented (e.g., using from three to five officers versus using from eight to 12 officers) or whether the officers remained at one location for an entire evening or moved to multiple locations.

Although checkpoints have considerable deterrence potential, they are limited in that many drunk drivers pass through roadblocks undetected. Research involving checkpoints where drivers not detained by police were subsequently tested for alcohol indicates that about one-half of the drivers with BAC's above the legal limit are not detained.

Passive alcohol sensors increase detection of drunk drivers in sobriety checkpoints. Passive sensors collect air from in front of a driver's face and can detect the presence of alcohol in the driver's breath. Use of these sensors is not believed to constitute a search under the fourth amendment and can be used by officers to establish probable cause that a driver has been drinking.

In one study, police detected 55 percent of drivers above the legal BAC limit when not using passive sensors, compared with 71 percent when using sensors. In addition, I.S. Jones and A.K. Lund found that when sensors are used, sober drivers are less likely to be erroneously suspected of alcohol use, and a lower percentage are asked to take field sobriety tests.

Perhaps the most extensive Statewide sobriety checkpoint program in the United States was implemented in Tennessee. From April 1994 through March 1995, more than 150,000 drivers were stopped at 900 checkpoints. The program was highly publicized on television. A quasi-experimental study revealed a 17-percent reduction in alcohol-related fatal crashes in Tennessee relative to five contiguous States during the same time period.

Preliminary breath testers have been available to police for more than 20 years. They are generally used after the police officer has conducted a field sobriety test and are useful in establishing probable cause for intoxication. States with laws permitting the use of preliminary breath tests at the roadside have been found to reduce nighttime fatal crashes significantly, even after the results were controlled analytically for a dozen potentially confounding variables such as unemployment, income, alcohol taxes, miles driven, and drinking.

Comprehensive Community Interventions

Enforcement is most likely to be effective in deterring alcohol-impaired driving if it is publicized, and it is most likely to be actively pursued by the police if they feel there is a strong demand for such action.

Citing its long-term success with other public health problems, the Institute of Medicine of the National Academy of Sciences has recommended comprehensive multistrategy community interventions to reduce alcohol-related health problems. For example, comprehensive community programs have achieved some success in reducing cardiovascular mortality and risks such as fat intake, blood pressure, smoking, and cholesterol level. Some recent community interventions have achieved minimal reductions in cardiovascular risks and prevalence of smoking; however, one study found significant declines in unintentional childhood injury.

The Saving Lives Program was implemented in March 1988. In each of six Massachusetts cities (combined population of 318,000), a full-time coordinator from the mayor's or city manager's office organized a task force of concerned private citizens and organizations and officials representing various city departments (e.g., school, health, police, and recreation). Each community received approximately $1 per inhabitant annually in program funds. Active task-force membership ranged from 20 to more than 100 persons, and an average of 50 organizations participated in each city. The communities not only attempted to reduce alcohol-impaired driving but also targeted other risky driving behaviors that alcohol-impaired drivers are more likely to engage in, such as speeding, red light violations, failure to yield to pedestrians in crosswalks, and failure to wear seatbelts.

Fatal crashes in program cities declined from 178 in the five years before the program to 120 during the five program years, a 25-percent decrease relative to the rest of Massachusetts. Likewise, fatal crashes involving alcohol declined by 42 percent relative to the rest of the State, from 69 in the five years preceding the program to 36 during the five years of the program. The number of fatally injured drivers with positive BAC's showed a decline of 47 percent in program cities, from 49 to 24. Visible injuries per 100 crashes declined by 5 percent, from 21.1 to 16.6. The proportion of vehicles observed speeding and the proportion of teenagers who reported driving after drinking were cut in half. The results clearly indicate that interventions organized by multiple city departments and private citizens can reduce driving after drinking, related driving risks, and traffic deaths and injuries. A major question is whether these changes can be sustained without support from the initial grant sources.

Comparing Community Programs

In the Community Trials Program, three experimental communities—one each in northern and southern California and one in South Carolina—were paired with comparison communities. The program incorporated community mobilization, media advocacy, training of alcoholic beverage servers, development of written serving policies by bars and restaurants, local zoning to reduce alcohol-outlet density, local enforcement of underage alcohol sales, alcohol-outlet clerk training in asking for age identification, police officer training, additional officer enforcement hours, use of passive alcohol sensors, and monthly sobriety checkpoints.

In program communities, relative to comparison communities,

changes included statistically significant program-related increases in media coverage of alcohol issues in local newspapers and on local television, a significant reduction in alcohol sales purchases to minors (i.e., sales were cut in half), and increased adoption of responsible server policies. Across all three program communities, a significant 10-percent postprogram reduction occurred in the numbers of SVN crashes per 100,000 population, with the greatest effects in the two California communities.

The results from these two studies reinforce findings from an earlier community study in which bartenders and counter clerks were trained to demonstrate the use of calculators to identify customer BAC levels based on customer weight and the number of drinks consumed. Television spots reinforced the messages. Roadside surveys conducted in both the intervention and the comparison communities before the program was implemented and six months after it was implemented revealed no differences between communities before the program was initiated. At the six-month survey, 5.8 percent of nighttime drivers in the program communities had BAC's of 0.05 percent or higher, compared with 11.1 percent in the comparison communities. This study demonstrates the potential for community interventions to change social norms about unacceptable drinking behavior before driving.

The Future of Drunk-Driving Research

Despite the progress made in reducing alcohol-related crashes since the early 1980's, the increase in such crashes in 1995 reminds us that important research questions persist.

Arrests for drunk driving have declined 26 percent since 1983. The reasons for those declines are not clear. Whether they reflect changes in attitudes among police command staff and patrol officers searching for DUI offenders or in the exercise of discretion in arresting offenders warrants exploration. The impact of reduced arrest rates on drivers' perceptions of the likelihood that alcohol-impaired drivers will be arrested also deserves scrutiny.

People who drive after drinking alcohol are more likely than other drivers to speed, run red lights, fail to yield to pedestrians, and fail to wear seatbelts. All of these behaviors heighten the risk of crashing or of being injured in a crash. The community program reported by R. Hingson, T. McGovern, J. Howland, T. Heeren, M. Winter, and R. Zakocs in Massachusetts targeted not only alcohol-impaired driving but also these related driving behaviors. Whether this strategy can succeed in other States warrants exploration. Massachusetts did not have a seatbelt law during that study period. Combining DUI enforcement with seatbelt checkpoints should be explored, particularly in States with primary seatbelt law enforcement that permit police to stop a vehicle because occupants are unbelted. Similarly, combining DUI and speed enforcement warrants study, because a high proportion of fatal crashes involving alcohol also involve excessive speed.

In 1995, 5,585 pedestrians died in alcohol-related crashes. Twenty percent of the drivers and 37 percent of the pedestrians had been drinking. Most attention on alcohol-involved traffic crashes has focused on drivers. N.E. Jones, C.F. Pieper, and L.S. Robertson found that adopting the MLDA of 21 reduced the number of both teenage driver and pedestrian deaths. Whether policy initiatives, such as lower legal BAC limits, alcohol taxes, zoning, or altering hours of sale, can influence pedestrian deaths deserves study.

H.L. Ross has indicated that most legal and community approaches to date have emphasized legal deterrence of alcohol-impaired driving. Less political discussion has focused on social causes of impaired driving. Ross insists that impaired driving can also be reduced by policies that decrease the overall use of cars as well as of alcohol. In addition, other strategies should be explored, including taxes and regulations on vehicles, gasoline, and alcohol sales; improved public transportation; and restrictions on driver age. Ross has also urged an examination of efforts to attenuate links between impairment, error, and crashes and between crashes, injuries, and deaths. Examples include improved highway and vehicle engineering and improved emergency medical services.

Since the early 1980's, legislative initiatives, such as the MLDA of 21, administrative license revocation, and lower legal BAC limits for youth and adults, have been independently associated with significant declines in alcohol-related traffic deaths. Active education and enforcement programs can enhance the beneficial effects of these laws. Furthermore, comprehensive community interventions that integrate the efforts of several city Government departments with those of concerned private citizens and organizations can substantially reduce alcohol-related traffic deaths, particularly if the programs also devote attention to other risky traffic behaviors disproportionately found among drinking drivers (e.g., speeding, running red lights, and failure to wear seatbelts). Nonetheless, although increases in the implementation of MLDA laws, traffic laws, and programs have helped cut alcohol-related traffic deaths by 31 percent nationwide, the bulk of the problem persists: Alcohol-related traffic deaths increased 4 percent in 1995, the first increase in a decade. Research is needed to explore ways to increase police enforcement of existing drunk-driving laws, to foster the passage of legislation known to reduce traffic injury and death, and to explore new ways to reduce alcohol-related traffic deaths, not only among drivers and passengers, but also among pedestrians. Furthermore, new ideas and new approaches will be needed if we are to make dramatic additional advances addressing this major public health problem.

GETTING HARD-CORE DRUNK DRIVERS OFF THE ROAD

John Lawn and Marion Blakey

Hard-core drunk drivers—repeat offenders who often have high blood alcohol concentrations—are responsible for more than half of all alcohol-related traffic fatalities. In the following article, John Lawn and Marion Blakey explore the measures that lawmakers are taking to solve the problem of hard-core drunk drivers. The authors explain that the federal government has passed highway funding legislation that offers funds to states that implement tougher laws against repeat offenders and redirects funds from states that fail to comply. The strategies implemented by the states vary, the authors report: Most states have some form of graduated penalty for repeat offenders, some use electronic monitoring, and others impound or confiscate the vehicles of hard-core drunk drivers. Lawn, a former administrator of the Drug Enforcement Administration, is the president and CEO of The Century Council, which combats drunk driving and is funded by the nation's distillers. Blakey is the coordinator of the National Hard-core Drunk Driver Project and a former administrator of the National Highway Traffic Safety Administration.

Hardcore drunk drivers are ravaging America's roadways. Look for them—next time there's a headline announcing a deadly alcohol-related crash, read on. Chances are the driver had a high blood alcohol concentration (BAC), was a repeat offender, or both. But unlike these drunk drivers, lawmakers are saying they've had enough.

The Problem

On local and national levels, officials are accelerating efforts to get hardcore drunk drivers off the streets. Since 1988 aggressive efforts to eradicate drunk driving have reduced alcohol-related fatalities in the United States by one-third. But statistics show almost no reduction in fatalities caused by hardcore drunk drivers—those motorists who repeatedly drive drunk, often with a high blood alcohol concentra-

Excerpted from "Getting Hardcore Drunk Drivers Off the Road," by John Lawn and Marion Blakey, *State Government News*, June/July 1998. Copyright 1998 The Council of State Governments. Reprinted with permission from *State Government News*.

tion, and who are highly resistant to changing their behavior.

Hardcore drunk drivers make up only a tiny percentage of drivers, but they are responsible for a huge number of crashes. For example, researchers, in a publication of the Traffic Injury Research Foundation in Ottawa, estimated that drivers with a blood alcohol concentration in excess of 0.15 percent are only 1 percent of all drivers on weekend nights, yet they are involved in nearly 50 percent of all fatal crashes at that time. Overall they account for more than half of all alcohol-related traffic fatalities. And traffic safety researchers attributed an estimated $33 billion in economic costs to hardcore drunk drivers involved in traffic fatalities in 1995.

Hardcore drunk driving presents a particularly difficult problem: It is difficult to understand, difficult to discourage and sometimes difficult to detect until lives are shattered. Yet solutions are evolving from new legislation, newly compiled data, promising strategies and innovative programs.

New Legislation and Promising Strategies

In 1997 and 1998, legislatures in 39 states across the country considered more than 275 bills—a record number—that address hardcore drunk driving. These bills include provisions for special driving-while-intoxicated (DWI) license plates, vehicle impoundment and forfeiture programs, and graduated penalties based on a BAC level.

At the national level, Congress in late May 1998 passed a major highway funding bill that affects state drunk driving policies and strategies. The new law prods the states to set 0.08 percent as the BAC level at which a driver is declared legally drunk and offers states major financial incentives to do so.

The new highway legislation also takes direct aim at hardcore drunk drivers. The bill offers states financial incentives to adopt tougher laws and more innovative sanctions to separate hardcore drunk drivers from their automobiles. Even better, the new legislation calls for special measures to cut back the number of people driving with a suspended license and to provide treatment for repeat offenders.

There also is a stick along with the financial carrots—the new law requires states to sentence repeat offenders to jail for a minimum of five days, or alternatively, at least 30 days of community service. For third and subsequent offenses the minimum penalty doubles. States that fail to comply would see 2 percent of their highway funds redirected.

Information on policies, laws and programs that effectively combat hardcore drunk driving and new survey information from all 50 states, the District of Columbia and U.S. territories are available from the National Hardcore Drunk Driver Project, established in 1997 by The Century Council, which is funded by the nation's leading distillers.

This new research and state data show that states are making genuine progress in confronting the problem of hardcore drunk driving:

Research shows that effective sanctions can have an enormous impact. Sanctions include electronic monitoring of repeat offenders; alcohol ignition interlock devices, which prevent a drunk driver from starting a car; vehicle impoundment, confiscation or forfeiture; and dedicated detention facilities.

Forty-nine states use some form of graduated penalties for repeat drunk drivers based on prior convictions. In addition, states are enacting stiffer penalties for drivers with high BACs. Experts say a system of escalating fines and penalties better identifies and processes hardcore drunk drivers.

More states are requiring an alcohol assessment of people convicted of drunk driving. The assessment identifies appropriate treatment measures and helps authorities deal with hardcore drunk drivers because it provides information about their drinking and driving habits. Research shows that treatment results in a significant drop in DWI recidivism.

A handful of states are developing effective DWI tracking systems. A 1997 report by the National Highway Traffic Safety Administration identifies effective systems and recommends that each state explore developing a comprehensive, judiciary-based system that eliminates the opportunity for hardcore drunk drivers to escape notice. South Dakota's Unified Judicial System provides coordinated and efficient processing and reporting of criminal drunk driving charges throughout the state. During a trial, the system provides complete, up-to-date information on an offender's court history, including payment of fines.

Although at times it seems like shadowboxing, legislators and policymakers are scoring some significant successes in their battles against hardcore drunk driving. New and pending legislation should further reduce the number of fatalities, injuries and damages that result from the irresponsible behavior of this small segment of the driving public.

The fight against hardcore drunk driving has been hamstrung by a lack of centralized information. To fill this void, The Century Council in 1997 created the National Hardcore Drunk Driver Project. The Council, a national not-for-profit organization, concentrates on the problems of drunk driving and underage drinking and is funded by America's leading distillers. The initiative is being guided by the recommendations of a panel of internationally recognized judges, researchers and professionals in the fields of alcohol abuse, law enforcement and traffic safety. The project will provide state and local policymakers with information to assist them in enacting laws and developing programs to reduce hardcore drunk driving. . . .

Cracking Down

The 1998 Wisconsin Legislature in May sent to Governor Tommy Thompson a bill to prescribe a five-year prison sentence for drivers with five or more convictions for operating a vehicle while intoxicated.

In North Carolina, a drunk driver received a sentence of life in prison in April 1998. The driver was found guilty of first-degree murder for striking and killing a four-year-old in another vehicle. The driver's blood alcohol level was 0.13 percent, which is above North Carolina's 0.08 percent legal limit. He had eight previous drunk driving convictions. (North Carolina defines a hardcore drunk driver as one with a BAC of 0.15 percent who repeatedly drives drunk.) The prosecutor relied on the state's rule that allows a murder charge for a death that occurs during commission of a felony. The driver was charged with felony assault for striking the vehicle in which the girl died.

Often a combination of tactics works best with hardcore drunk drivers:

Alcohol ignition interlock devices, used in at least 37 states, can significantly reduce recidivism, at least while the restriction is in place. The purpose is to prevent an offender who has consumed alcohol from driving. The device measures alcohol concentration in the breath and is attached to the vehicle's ignition system. The driver must blow into the device before the car will start. If the alcohol in the driver's breath is above the predetermined level, the vehicle will not start. About 24,000 devices are installed in the United States.

A 1997 study of multiple offenders in Maryland found that being in an interlock program reduced an individual's risk of recidivism within the first year by about 65 percent.

Electronic monitoring of repeat offenders, often coupled with house arrest, is permitted in 33 states and the District of Columbia. Under this sanction, offenders are under court order to be at home during specified hours. The offender wears an electronic device or is supervised by random telephone monitoring. The electronic monitoring/home detention program in Los Angeles has reduced the recidivism rate for offenders by about 33 percent.

Impoundment involves seizing and storing the DWI offender's vehicle in a compound. Impoundment programs have gained in popularity and are used in 12 states. San Francisco's Traffic Offender Program provides for a 30-day impoundment of any vehicle driven by a person with a suspended or revoked license, or by a person who has never been issued a license. Although the program is not aimed solely at drunk driving offenders, safety officials think the law has had a tremendous impact on drunk driving. In the program's first two years, it produced a 63 percent drop in alcohol-related fatal and injury collisions. San Francisco's vehicle impoundment program collected $1.5 million in violator-paid administrative fees in 1995 and 1996, an amount program administrators consider break-even.

Dedicated Detention Facilities, which house multiple DWI offenders, are a sentencing alternative that can help ease prison overcrowding. These confinement facilities provide supervised alcohol treatment services and have been shown to reduce recidivism. Detention usually ranges from two weeks to 90 days. Such facilities are in operation in several locations including Baltimore County, Maryland; Jamaica Plain, Massachusetts; and Suffolk County, New York.

Organizations That Fight Teen Drunk Driving

Jim Travisano

In the following article, author Jim Travisano examines some of the grassroots organizations that work to solve the problem of teens who drive while drunk. He writes that Mothers Against Drunk Driving (MADD) works closely with young people to combat underage drinking. The organization's annual MADD National Youth Summit to Prevent Underage Drinking is particularly designed to reach teenagers, he explains. In addition, MADD has been successful in lobbying efforts to raise the legal drinking age to twenty-one nationwide, Travisano maintains. The author also explores the efforts of Students Against Destructive Decisions (SADD), an organization of students who work to discourage teen drunk driving through a variety of measures, such as staging mock alcohol-related car crashes. Travisano is the communications director for the McIntire School of Commerce at the University of Virginia in Charlottesville.

When Diana, Princess of Wales, was killed in a car crash on August 31, 1997, millions around the world mourned her publicly, and her two children were left to grow up without a mother. Two others in the car also were killed.

The tragedy might never have happened if the driver of the car had been sober. But tests revealed he had a blood alcohol content three times higher than the legal limit in France. What's more, further tests found that he had traces of antidepressant drugs in his system. Combined with alcohol, these drugs can slow reaction time.

Absolutely no one is immune from the devastating effects of drunk driving. In fact, more than 2,000 people age 16 to 20 die every year in vehicle crashes involving a drunk driver.

The good news is young people are fighting back against drunk drivers—and often they're winning! The number of intoxicated young drivers in fatal crashes dropped more than 14 percent from 1986 to 1996. That's the largest decrease for *any* age group.

Reprinted from "For Safety's Sake . . . Join the Club," by Jim Travisano, *Current Health 2*, December 1997. Special permission granted by *Current Health 2*®, published and copyrighted by Weekly Reader Corporation. All rights reserved.

Avoiding crashes is no accident. One of the ways young people are winning the war against drinking and driving is through safety clubs, including Mothers Against Drunk Driving (MADD), Students Against Destructive Decisions (SADD—the organization was formerly known as Students Against Drunk Driving), and the National Student Safety Program (NSSP).

Mothers Against Drunk Driving

Thirteen-year-old Cari Lightner was walking down a quiet street in Fair Oaks, California. Moments later, she was killed instantly by a car driven by a drunk driver. The car hit Cari with such force that she was thrown more than 120 feet. The driver sped away.

Cari's mother, Candy Lightner, found out that the driver had several prior drunk-driving convictions—and was likely to serve little, if any, jail time for the death of her daughter.

Her response was to form Mothers Against Drunk Driving, which soon became known as MADD. Her one-woman crusade grew into an organization with 3 million members nationwide. MADD has changed attitudes and saved lives.

Perhaps one of MADD's greatest accomplishments has been helping to raise the drinking age to 21 in all 50 states—a change that experts say saves 800 lives a year. But MADD isn't just for adults.

In 1996, MADD announced a new partnership with young people to combat the number-one drug problem among America's youth: alcohol. The name of the program is Youth in Action. Teams of young people work with MADD adult partners to change the climate that suggests that underage drinking is an acceptable choice.

One facet of the program is the annual MADD National Youth Summit to Prevent Underage Drinking. During the first summit held in May 1997, 435 high school students—one from each U.S. congressional district or U.S. territory—met in Washington, D.C., for four days to share their concerns about underage drinking—and to help make a difference with policy makers and elected officials.

"I loved getting together with people from different states, speaking our minds and having a voice," said delegate Tara Skimmer from Utah.

MADD also sponsors a national poster/essay contest for young people. The theme for 1997 was My World, My Choice, No Alcohol. First place winner Michael Krause II wrote in part:

> Now it was graduation. To celebrate, he and his friends partied. They were feeling great, so why not have a beer or two or three? or six? Or . . . well, they lost count. The boy stumbled to the car to drive the crew home. . . . In one moment of screeching brakes and grinding metal, his castle was demolished. The beach was swept clean, and the only thing

left of the boy, with the world at his fingertips, were pictures and memories.

Students Against Destructive Decisions

SADD was created in 1982 by Robert Anastas, a high school hockey coach, when two of his players died in separate car crashes. SADD is now an international organization with 4 million members and 20,000 chapters.

SADD activities are varied—often they're designed by students themselves. Nikki Finch, 18, president of her local SADD chapter in Palma Ceia, Florida, has helped stage such events and was voted Student of the Year by her SADD peers. A key reason she won the award was her enthusiastic approach to recruiting fellow students. She turned a local group of what one teacher described as "40 or so wishy-washy members" into a group of 180 dedicated kids who put together such events as a mock fatal alcohol-related crash.

During such an event, real emergency equipment and personnel are present. Tools such as the "jaws of life," back boards, and cervical collars are used to extricate the "victims," who are transported by ambulance. A hearse is used to pick up the "dead" student. The simulation is complete when police officers test the young driver for intoxication—and then arrest him and take him away.

"A lot of my peers drink, and the problem is they don't drink socially. They drink to get drunk," Nikki says. "Drunk driving deaths are so preventable—they're not an accident. If even one young person dies, it's one too many."

THE AUTOMOBILE FORFEITURE DEBATE

Alexandra Varney McDonald

In the following article, journalist Alexandra Varney McDonald reports on one of the most controversial programs in the fight against drunk driving: automobile forfeiture. According to McDonald, supporters maintain that confiscating the vehicles of drunk drivers will help to reduce the incidence of drunk driving and prevent serious accidents. They argue that automobile forfeiture has already been proven effective against drug dealers and others who use their vehicles in the furtherance of their crimes, the author explains. However, she writes, critics of the policy claim that it is unconstitutional because it allows the authorities to confiscate vehicles before the drivers are found innocent or guilty of drunk driving. McDonald also states that critics believe drivers are punished arbitrarily and unfairly under this program because some of the confiscated vehicles are worth much more than others.

Although U.S. Representative Earl Blumenauer of Oregon thinks New York City's automobile forfeiture policy is extreme, he likes it just the same.

Blumenauer was planning in June 1999 to reintroduce federal legislation that would encourage states to institute auto forfeiture in multiple-offense, drunk-driving cases.

Raising the stakes against intoxicated drivers, on February 22, 1999, New York City began taking the vehicles of those charged with drunk driving for the first time. Other jurisdictions have similar policies in place for repeat offenders.

A Controversial Policy

Because forfeiture is a civil proceeding with a lesser burden of proof, defendants could lose their cars even if they are found not guilty on the drunk-driving charge. As such, Mayor Rudolph Giuliani's policy has garnered widespread publicity, some measure of criticism and a lawsuit.

"One of the positive things that come out of the attention given to New York City," says Blumenauer, "is that people may think it's an extreme application, but it puts the issue on the radar screen and makes what I'm talking about seem more tame and reasonable."

Unlike Giuliani's policy, the federal bill would apply only to repeat offenders. And, Blumenauer says, mechanisms would be in place to protect third-party owners of vehicles, if, say, a car is borrowed or belongs to a rental or leasing company.

The federal bill would encourage states to institute auto forfeiture by including it as one of the options they can choose to qualify for federal highway safety funds.

The New York program uses a city law allowing police to impound and impose forfeiture of property used as an instrumentality in the commission of a crime. In the first month of the policy, 164 vehicles were seized.

Other jurisdictions may follow New York City's lead. Just weeks into the program, it had prompted at least 50 inquiries, say representatives of the mayor's office. The callers represented various governmental bodies in such diverse locales as California, Florida, Illinois, Louisiana, Massachusetts, Texas, Austria, Canada and France.

Among their questions: Is this new weapon against the societal problem of drunk driving legal? New York City officials answer in the affirmative. They say the same law has been applied and upheld for years to seize the vehicles of drug dealers and persons soliciting prostitutes who use their vehicles in furtherance of the crimes.

"This is a different application of the exact same laws," says Daniel S. Connolly, special counsel to the city's corporation counsel. "Their legality has already been well-established."

Daniel C. Richman, a professor at Fordham law school in New York City, believes the policy raises many moral issues, but for the most part, he agrees that the constitutional issues have already been decided.

"This enforcement tactic is quite old," says Richman. "It's only now that it's being applied in a context that impacts more middle-class people that it seems to raise opposition. It's not a very large jump to go from the application in the drug context to the application in the drunk-driving context."

Questioning the Policy's Constitutionality

Norman Siegel, executive director of the New York Civil Liberties Union (NYCLU), disagrees, calling the policy unlawful and unconstitutional. The NYCLU in March 1999 filed a class action suit seeking to overturn it. [On May 19, 1999, the New York Superior Court ruled against the NYCLU, finding the forfeiture policy constitutional.]

Three arguments are made in the suit. First, it says only the state has the authority to impose forfeiture as a punishment for a first-time drunk-driving offense. Second, it says the policy deprives people of their property without due process. Third, it argues that the policy could lead to "excessive and disproportionate punishment."

In 1998, the U.S. Supreme Court ruled in *U.S. v. Bajakajian* that the government cannot seize a person's property if the value is "grossly disproportional" to the gravity of the offense.

Based on that case, a driver who loses a car under New York's policy might argue the initiative doles out punishment arbitrarily. One driver may lose a car worth only a few hundred dollars, while another may lose one worth tens of thousands of dollars.

New York City's Connolly retorts that no automobile is worth more than the potential harm of drunk driving.

Blumenauer appreciates the rigorous debate, if only because it will draw more attention to what he considers the bigger federal picture. "I would be perfectly happy if every jurisdiction applied forfeiture for repeat drunk drivers," he says.

THE IGNITION INTERLOCK PROGRAM

Michael Weinrath

Ignition interlock devices prevent drivers from operating their vehicles when they are drunk but permit them to drive when sober. Some jurisdictions have instituted programs in which these devices are installed in vehicles of individuals who have been arrested for driving under the influence of alcohol. In the following selection, Michael Weinrath evaluates the effectiveness of the ignition interlock program in Alberta, Canada. According to Weinrath, the ignition interlock program was successful: Individuals who participated in this program were less likely to drive drunk, receive a serious driving violation, or be involved in an accident than were those offenders who took part in different programs. Weinrath is an instructor in the department of sociology at the University of Alberta in Edmonton.

In both Canada and the United States, fully 40% to 50% of all traffic fatalities are alcohol related, and despite a decline in overall drinking and driving, the costs of this behavior continue to be high. In the face of this continuing social problem, government policies are increasingly directed at reducing recidivism, particularly for chronic cases. However, policy direction is lacking, because researchers have been unable to identify effective strategies to reduce recidivism.

Traditional Solutions

Punitive sanctions and treatment programs have had mixed results. License suspension and jail terms have been imposed to deter and incapacitate impaired drivers. Treatment interventions have attempted to change offender behavior through required attendance at rehabilitation programs, such as alcohol counseling. License suspension is generally acknowledged as the most effective sanction, even though some of the incapacitation effects may be spurious. That is, investigators have discovered that some suspended drivers continue to drive, although their efforts to avoid detection do appear to result in more prudent driving behavior. As part of "get tough" campaigns against drunk drivers, the use of custodial sanctions has increased

Excerpted from "The Ignition Interlock Program for Drunk Drivers: A Multivariate Test," by Michael Weinrath, *Crime & Delinquency*, vol. 41, no. 1 (January 1997), pp. 42–59. Copyright © 1997 Sage Publications, Inc. Reprinted by permission of Sage Publications, Inc.

over the last decade, with the aim of reducing drunk driving through individual deterrence. Yet the effects of incarceration have been found to be equivocal at best, which is of particular concern when the high costs and intrusiveness of custody are considered. The deterrent effects of incarceration are difficult to assess because "short and sharp" mandatory jail terms may go unserved. Legislators generally fail to commit resources for more prison beds when passing tough drunk-driving laws and as a consequence, impaired drivers are turned away from jail. When county facilities become overcrowded, administrators give greater priority to predatory offenders and those awaiting trial.

There is an ongoing debate in the traffic safety field over the relative effectiveness of punitive sanctions versus rehabilitation programs. In the short term, compared to treatment, license suspension is more effective in reducing drunk-driving recidivism and subsequent collisions. However, the impact of taking away a driver's license appears to diminish over time, and alcohol rehabilitation programs are more effective in the long term in reducing repeat drunk driving. Despite the greater long-term benefits of treatment programs and the relative ineffectiveness of jail terms, rehabilitation has generally not shown large effects. A recent meta-evaluation, focusing on reasonably well designed evaluations, found that—compared to jail, fines, or no treatment—treatment programs reduced recidivism by a modest 8% to 9%.

Given the lack of strong effects from traditional interventions and growing concern over the persistent drinking driver, practitioners and scholars have proposed alternative driving under the influence (DUI) interventions. Some of these are *individual based,* such as intermediate sanctions. To reduce reliance on costly incarceration, programs using some combination of treatment, punishment, and surveillance—such as probation, house arrest, and/or electronic monitoring—have been developed. Individual-based sanctions rely on an assumption that intervention can effect a behavioral change in individuals. Other programs are *vehicle based,* such as vehicle impoundment for suspended drivers, seizure or restriction of offender license plates, and imposition of the ignition interlock device. These programs assume that the intervention (no vehicle, no license plate, car will not start if drinking) will incapacitate or limit the driver's ability to drive while drunk. Little is yet known about the use of individual-based alternative sanctions using multiple interventions, although earlier studies of probation and electronic monitoring have provided promising results. Vehicle impoundment appears limited by legal difficulties in confiscation; the costs of vehicle storage; and offenders driving cars owned by spouse, family, or friends, who typically have their vehicles returned because they claim to have been unaware that the offender was driving.

Using Ignition Interlock to Reduce Recidivism

The ignition interlock program, a high-tech intervention making use of new technology, has been proposed as a means to reduce DUI recidivism for even the most difficult, chronic cases. Ignition interlock prevents operation of a vehicle when an individual is drunk but still allows driving when the operator is sober. It provides education by requiring the driver to change life habits related to drinking and driving. As a behavioral reinforcer, it provides consistent and immediate feedback on inappropriate alcohol consumption. The vehicle will not start in any situation where an individual has imbibed too much. Ignition interlock performs an additional deterrent function akin to fines, license suspension, and custody, through payment of program fees by the offender. Some critics argue that use of such devices constitutes a "largely negative program." Yet, when viewed against lengthy periods of license suspension, residential treatment, or incarceration, ignition interlock presents a most attractive alternative. In most programs, participants can live a normal life, with few restrictions on movement and ample opportunity for employment and support of dependents.

The present evaluation of an ignition interlock program operated in Alberta, Canada since 1990, addresses several questions. Is the ignition interlock program effective in reducing impaired driving recidivism? Does it have an impact on more serious, persistent impaired drivers? Finally, does the program continue to be effective, even after the interlock device is removed? . . .

As of January 1997, Alberta is the only Canadian province using interlock. Repeat license suspensions for high-risk and impaired drivers are administered by the Alberta Driver Control Board (DCB), which consists of two full-time civil servants and 30 community members appointed by the legislature. To help manage impaired drivers, the DCB began a pilot program involving the ignition interlock device in 1990, with 48 cases considered for use that year. The ignition interlock device is required before license reinstatement for drunk drivers under certain circumstances. Imposition of the device may result in licenses being returned earlier for first or second offenders. In other situations, interlock may be a mandated requirement for serious multiple repeat impaired drivers before any type of license reinstatement. To start his or her car, the driver must blow into the device, mounted on the dashboard, and blow randomly each hour after that to keep the vehicle running. Any reading of .04 milligrams of alcohol per 100 milliliters of blood will prevent the automobile from starting or continuing to operate. The DCB receives a monthly report of each participant's interlock Breathalyzer™ readings to help monitor cases. The board administrator may suspend drivers whose Breathalyzer™ readings show a pattern of alcohol abuse. The in-car device is installed and managed by a private firm, Guardian Interlock.

Installation costs the driver $133.75, followed by a monthly mainte-nance fee of $101.65.

After the pilot program, regular use of the ignition interlock pro-gram by board members increased slowly. The interlock device was not uniformly assigned throughout the province during the pro-gram's first few years of operation. Its use varied between board mem-bers and by region. More stringent policy guidelines have been put in place, and the ignition interlock program is presently used exten-sively by all board members: 550 cases were active in March 1995.

The Study's Participants

For the ignition interlock program evaluation, a disproportionate strat-ified random sample of license-suspended Alberta impaired drivers was selected from computer files covering the years 1989–94. The sample comprised 994 offenders age 20 and older, including all female drunk drivers from those years (125), a random selection of 701 male drivers (sampling frame of 4,394), and 189 ignition interlock cases (sampling frame of 441) from the years 1990–94. Subsequent reclassification resulted in a final breakdown of 168 ignition interlock program cases and 826 impaired drivers in the comparison group. . . .

Observed differences in recidivism rates between ignition interlock program participants and the comparison group were striking. Only 10% of the ignition interlock cases recorded a new impaired-driving conviction, compared with 25% of the other high-risk drivers. For new high-risk driving violations, 2.4% of the interlock program cases reoffended, compared with 13.7% of the comparison group. Injury collision outcomes showed a similar pattern: Only 1% of the ignition interlock cases were involved in an injury collision, compared with 7% of the other high-risk drivers. Considered as odds, ignition inter-lock cases were almost 3 times *less likely* than the comparison group to drink and drive again. Program participants were 6.5 times less likely to record a new serious driving violation and about 5.8 times less likely to be involved in an injury collision. On the face of it, igni-tion interlock appeared to substantially reduce recidivism. . . .

Chronic Drunk Drivers

Policymakers often focus on hard-core cases. Are the effects of igni-tion interlock more or less pronounced for chronic drunk drivers? The study group of 994 ignition interlock and comparison group drunk drivers had driving records that were serious enough to warrant appearance before the DCB, but the sample still included many dri-vers with one or two prior drunk-driving convictions. To assess pro-gram effects for more chronic cases, recidivism outcomes were deter-mined for impaired drivers with three or more prior DUI convictions. Use of three priors to define chronic or hard-core impaired drivers is subject to a degree of measurement error, given undetected impaired-driving episodes, and debates within the addictions field over accurate definitions of problem drinkers versus seriously dependent drinkers. Lacking self-report data, it was felt that the certainty of 90 days' incarceration in Canada on the third impaired-driving conviction was a reasonable indicator of difficulty or reluctance to change behavior. More pragmatically, the use of three priors allowed for the retention of sufficient program and comparison cases for analysis. Using four or five DUI priors would shrink the available pool for analysis and also limit the generalizabilty of the data to a select group of very hard-core cases. . . .

Substantial program effects for ignition interlock were again observed for recidivism outcomes. Ignition interlock cases were far less likely to drink and drive again (11% to 28%), to commit a new driving offense (2.4% to 10.8%), or to become involved in an injury collision (1.2% to 4.6%). The odds of success for ignition interlock cases were consistent with those for DUI recidivism (2.95 all impaired drivers to 3.10 for chronic). Differences for high-risk driving offenses (6.50 to 4.86) and injury collision (5.81 to 3.91) were somewhat smaller but still highly favored program participants. . . .

Survival Rates

Survival rates estimated the number of reinstated drivers who had not reoffended or who had "survived" to various follow-up intervals (i.e., no DUI to 6 months, 12 months, 18 months, etc.). Survival rates provided another means of gauging the relative effectiveness of DUI sanctions on recidivism, better informing policy and program design. . . . The period of 24 months was chosen to ensure a reasonable follow-up period while maintaining sample size.

At 6 months, 93% of the comparison group had not recidivated, compared with 99% of ignition interlock cases. By 12 months, survival rates were 87% for comparison cases and 95% for interlock participants, and at the 18-month mark, 84% of the comparison group still survived compared with 93% of interlock. Finally, at 24 months, only 81% of the comparison group remained successful, compared with 91% of interlock cases. The 10% difference in survival rates at the 2-year mark again demonstrated the tangible impact of the ignition interlock program.

Participation in the ignition interlock program increased the probability of survival, but how much of the success of interlock was due to the device in the car (incapacitation or deterrence effect) versus a post-program learning (rehabilitative) effect? Survival rates were estimated for program cases for the 15-month period *after* removal of the ignition interlock and contrasted against the license-reinstated comparison group. Because of data limitations, a longer follow-up period for interlock participants was not possible without losing too many cases.

Results again showed lower recidivism rates for offenders who were involved in the ignition interlock program. Over the first 6 months, survival rates were roughly even (97% program, 95% comparison), but differences increased over time. By 9 months, the program group survival rate was 4% better, and by 12 months it was 5% better. At the end of 15 months, the DUI survival rate was 92% for ignition interlock cases compared with 87% for the comparison group: This 5% difference provided some modest support for a rehabilitative program effect. The 10% difference in survival rates between program and comparison groups at 24 months was statistically significant, as was the 5% difference for "after-interlock" and comparison cases. . . .

A Successful Program

For the Alberta program, net of the effects of other risk factors, participation in an ignition interlock program reduced the likelihood of recidivism for impaired driving, high-risk driving, and injury collisions. When compared with a group who received only license suspensions, ignition interlock program participants were twice as likely to successfully avoid repeat drunk driving. Ignition interlock cases were 4.4 times less likely to record a new serious driving violation and 3.9 times less likely to be involved in an injury collision. Similar program effects were observed for a subsample of chronic impaired drivers. Program effects for injury collisions were particularly noteworthy, as these crashes inflict the most long-term pain and suffering, both fiscally and emotionally. Comparisons of lifetime medical, law enforcement, motor vehicle agency, and insurance cost of crashes place average property collisions at only $2,000 and minor injuries at $5,000. Lifetime costs for major injuries rank highest at $515,000.

Survival rates for licensed reinstated drivers displayed evidence of program effectiveness, even after the ignition interlock device was removed. A difference of 10% in DUI recidivism at the 24-month mark indicated overall program effectiveness, whereas a 5% difference at the 15-month mark for after-interlock cases showed some evidence of postprogram treatment effects. Ignition interlock succeeded as both a vehicle-based and individual-based sanction. The overall benefits of ignition interlock appear to warrant continued operation of the program in Alberta.

Despite statistical significance, was the 5% DUI survival rate improvement, after the ignition interlock device was removed, "large enough?" The decline in effectiveness after the interlock was removed suggests that longer periods on ignition interlock would have increased survival rates. Whether program assignment periods increase significantly or modestly, the extent of increases must weigh costs to participants against public safety benefits.

The results of this evaluation were more supportive of ignition interlock than evaluations conducted in Ohio and California and much more consistently positive than outcomes observed in Oregon.

Comparison of programs was difficult, because factors affecting road safety varied among jurisdictions (e.g., demographic factors, miles driven, urban/rural concentrations, topography). Yet a potentially confounding factor, program operation, also offered a plausible explanation for the Alberta ignition interlock program's greater success. There were several operational differences between Alberta and Oregon interlock programs. Oregon used a voluntary 6-month interlock period for all drivers who wished their licenses back before the end of a 3-year suspension. Alberta provided a similar program option for drivers with one and usually two DUI convictions, but the DCB also used the program extensively for chronic repeat cases who were license suspended for indeterminate periods. Ignition interlock was (and remains) part of a larger assessment process by the DCB, which can vary the length of program assignment for more serious cases and require offenders to take driver education and alcohol/drug programs. Drivers who continue to drink and fail their ignition interlock Breathalyzer™ test too often may be suspended or have their program length extended. Put simply, the success of Alberta's program likely was due to more individualized management of impaired drivers than was the case in Oregon and perhaps other programs. Reduction of recidivism through better matching of program interventions to individuals has found increasing support in the impaired-driving literature.

USING THE MEDIA TO CHANGE DRUNK DRIVING POLICIES

William DeJong

William DeJong is a professor at the Harvard School of Public Health in Boston, Massachusetts, and a member of Mothers Against Drunk Driving (MADD). In the following selection, DeJong explains that media advocacy can be very useful in educating the public about social issues such as drunk driving. However, he warns that organizations must be careful when choosing such a strategy because it can backfire in a variety of ways. As an example, DeJong discusses the problems that MADD's state branch in Massachusetts faced when it chose to use media advocacy to promote its legislative agenda. The author explains that MADD Massachusetts was specifically upset with a state senator who repeatedly opposed and blocked legislation that the organization supported. The group resorted to a confrontational media strategy to raise public awareness about the senator's actions, DeJong writes. At first MADD Massachusetts gained the publicity they wanted on this issue, he reveals, but soon many members of the press and public began to view the group's tactics as overzealous and negative. The negative media campaign actually damaged MADD's public image as a positive force for change, DeJong concludes.

Since 1986, the citizen advocates of Mothers Against Drunk Driving (MADD) had been frustrated by Massachusetts state Senator Ed Burke, a Democrat from the Boston suburb of Framingham. With the apparent acquiescence of Senate President William M. Bulger, a Democrat from Boston, Burke had been able to block a number of bills that were important to MADD's membership. To MADD's dismay, no important drunk driving legislation had been passed in the Commonwealth since the 1986 Safe Roads Act.

In 1991, the Massachusetts legislature once again considered the so-called "admissibility bill," which would make it possible for a

Excerpted from "MADD Massachusetts Versus Senator Burke: A Media Advocacy Case Study," by William DeJong, *Health Education Quarterly*, vol. 23, no. 3 (August 1996), pp. 318–29. Copyright © 1996 by SOPHE. Reprinted by permission of Sage Publications, Inc.

drunk driving defendant's refusal to take a breathalyzer test to be admitted as evidence in a criminal trial. This is the law in most states, and the U.S. Supreme Court had ruled that a similar measure in South Dakota was constitutional. Even so, Burke was adamantly opposed, and he resorted to a series of end-of-session maneuvers to keep the admissibility bill from becoming law.

MADD Massachusetts' state leadership responded with anger. Having worked for years behind the scenes, MADD now made its displeasure with Burke publicly known. Nothing angers MADD's advocates more than loopholes in the law that protect drunk driving offenders from the consequences of their actions, except perhaps a state legislator who plays parliamentary games to prevent those loopholes from being closed.

Using Media Advocacy

The story of MADD versus Burke is a cautionary tale for volunteer organizations that want to turn to the airwaves to advance their causes. MADD eventually got its way on the admissibility bill, but the victory came at great cost. Originally, MADD Massachusetts had identified other more important legislative priorities and had launched a media plan to put its proposals on the public agenda. The dispute with Burke not only threw that plan off course, it also exposed deep schisms within MADD Massachusetts regarding the nature and purpose of the organization and the appropriateness of using confrontational media strategies to advance its agenda. Paralyzed by the lack of consensus among its grassroots membership, MADD Massachusetts was rendered a far less effective advocate for policy change.

Media advocacy represents a new paradigm in the field of public health, one in which health educators focus on using the media to galvanize political action and change. As L. Wallack, L. Dorfman, D. Jernigan, and M. Themba describe it, media advocacy is about *education*, helping move public discourse from a focus on individual blame to a more proper focus on societal conditions and institutional arrangements that are at the root of public health problems. Media advocacy is also about *power*, with communities using their voice to define and make their concerns known and controlling media images and symbols to build support for changes in public policy.

As discussed by Wallack and his colleagues, media advocates have to understand the forces that shape how the mass media cover social issues. Fundamental to that understanding is the fact that news programs must draw audiences, and to do that they must entertain. For this reason, the news often is presented through stories of individual victimization or conflict. Once the news media begin to pay attention, advocates are faced with the challenge of selecting images, words, and symbols to frame the problem from their perspective. Media advocacy, then, often is a battle over competing *frames*.

The Internal Debate

MADD was founded in 1980 in Sacramento, California, by Candy Lightner, whose young daughter was killed by a repeat drunk driving offender. MADD has been noisy and effective. As a result, drunk driving no longer is the subject of easy jokes but instead is viewed as a serious public danger. This change in public attitude, coupled with hundreds of tougher antidrunk driving laws, has led to a drop in alcohol-related fatalities from 25,165 in 1982 to 17,699 in 1992.

The image of the "angry mother" still predominates in the public's view of MADD, but the organization is also credited with saving many lives. Polls consistently have shown that MADD has among the highest name recognition and highest favorability ratings of any nonprofit organization in the United States. A 1993 Gallup poll showed, for example, that when asked to name an organization working to stop drunk driving, 71% cited MADD. More recently, MADD was identified in a national survey as America's favorite charitable cause.

MADD's public service advertising has been consistent with its public image of earnestness and caring. Among MADD's most visible media events is Project Red Ribbon, an annual public awareness campaign held during the December holiday period. With the slogan, "Tie One On for Safety," actress Connie Sellecca asks Americans each year to tie red ribbons to their cars as a symbol of their commitment to drive sober.

MADD's image and its credibility are a valuable resource, which can be used to advantage as the organization pushes for policy change. MADD's political capital is not inexhaustible, however, and it must be spent wisely. Even though MADD's public image is generally positive, people do have ambivalent feelings about any public interest group such as MADD that wields political influence. And when a group has a name like "MADD," charges of zealotry can stick. This fact raises serious debate among MADD's volunteers about the use of confrontational tactics that might tarnish the organization's public image and threaten its ties with the media, corporate sponsors, and sympathetic politicians. The structure of this debate is instructive.

MADD's Agenda

In many ways, MADD seems ideally suited for media advocacy work. Staffed mostly by volunteers, many of whom lost loved ones in alcohol-related traffic crashes, MADD speaks with genuine moral authority. Moreover, while part of MADD's legislative agenda is designed to ensure that convicted drunk drivers are punished, much of the agenda focuses on prevention through general deterrence, a strategy that seeks to change the environment in which people make decisions about their drinking and driving behavior. Much of MADD's success in advancing this agenda can be attributed to its sophisticated use of the media.

Other factors mitigate against MADD being an effective media advocate. Many of MADD's grassroots members do not know MADD's history of successful legislative advocacy, nor do they appreciate the need for confrontational media strategies to advance the organization's agenda. For these volunteers, public education is the thing, and they work hard each year to make Project Red Ribbon and other public awareness campaigns big successes. Being a media advocate, which can mean being controversial, does not fit their style or their image of MADD.

Regretfully, the fact that this difference of opinion existed was not well understood by the leadership of MADD Massachusetts as it pursued its legislative agenda in 1991.

In 1990, MADD National, based in Irving, Texas, announced an ambitious plan for the nation's fight against drunk driving: reducing the proportion of alcohol-related traffic fatalities by 20% by the year 2000. Key to this plan was a comprehensive statement of legislative priorities.

Among the more important measures MADD supports is reducing the per se limit that defines intoxicated driving from the current level of .10% to .08% BAC (blood alcohol concentration) for adults and to .02% BAC for minors. Legislation is required in each of the states to put these changes into effect.

Taking its lead from MADD National, the organization's state office in Massachusetts put .08/.02 at the top of its legislative priorities for 1991. Kay Dudley, the state chairperson for MADD, and William A. Caplin, who headed the legislative committee, prepared to work quietly behind the scenes to press for the new laws.

The International Candlelight Vigil

MADD's International Candlelight Vigil is an annual event held each December as a remembrance for the victims of drunk driving. In 1991, MADD National chose MADD Massachusetts to host the vigil. Dudley and other state MADD leaders immediately recognized that local news media coverage of the vigil offered the perfect opportunity to put .08/.02 on the public agenda.

Critical to this effort was a media luncheon that MADD hosted on the afternoon prior to the vigil. Typically, the luncheon, like the vigil itself, is used to generate victim-oriented news stories, and news reporters are invited to interview victims from across the country who are in attendance. This time, however, MADD Massachusetts structured the entire luncheon to help make the case for lower BAC limits.

Two early decisions were made to encourage reporters and news editors to attend the luncheon. First, Peter Meade, an on-air radio personality with WBZ-AM, was invited to host the luncheon. Meade had been outspoken about the need for tougher drunk driving laws ever since Dennis Kauff, a reporter from WB Z-TV, had been killed by a drunk driver in 1985. Meade eagerly agreed to host the luncheon.

Second, MADD Massachusetts approached Kauff's widow, Paula Childs, to ask if MADD could create a news reporting award in honor of her husband. Childs, a news reporter with a rival television station and a MADD supporter, immediately recognized the importance of the award and gave her consent. Meade, in turn, asked WBZ-TV news anchorman John Henning to make the award presentation at the media luncheon.

The Kauff Award was presented to reporter Hank Phillippi Ryan of WHDH-TV in Boston for her series, "One Too Many," which took a hard look at the drunk driving laws in Massachusetts and their lax enforcement. In an excerpt played at the luncheon, a woman news producer drank measured amounts of alcohol and then attempted to drive a car on a test course, which served to demonstrate vividly that driving ability is severely impaired at .08% BAC.

Pushing to Lower the Legal Limit

Lieutenant Governor Paul Cellucci also attended the media luncheon to read a proclamation from Governor William F. Weld and to promote the governor's new drunk driving bill, especially its provision for lowering the legal BAC limit for adults to .08%. MADD Massachusetts had hoped that the lieutenant governor would also announce support for a .02% BAC limit for minors, but that was not yet part of the governor's proposed package, and the lieutenant governor declined.

Yet another key to the luncheon was a presentation by Ralph Hingson from Boston University's School of Public Health on the experience of other states that had installed a per se limit of .08% BAC and lower limits for youths.

The vigil itself was held that evening at the John F. Kennedy Memorial Library. It was a highly emotional event, and with family members lighting candles in memory of their loved ones lost to drunk driving, it was a natural for television coverage. For strategic reasons, MADD Massachusetts invited Bulger, the senate president, to make a brief presentation at the vigil.

MADD Massachusetts' strategy for putting .08/.02 on the state public agenda paid off. The *Boston Globe*'s story about the vigil included a full discussion of MADD's legislative agenda, as did stories in other Boston-area newspapers and on WHDH-TV.

On the day after the vigil, MADD National launched a caravan (called the "CaringVan") from Boston to Washington, D.C., which would arrive for a "Red Ribbon Rally" to open that year's observances for National Drunk and Drugged Driving Awareness Week. Along the route, which included several major media markets, MADD officials visited the sites of recent drunk driving crashes and dedicated plaques to the victims. The launch of the CaringVan also made the Boston television news.

The local news coverage accomplished two additional objectives. First, it reminded the public that the drunk driving problem in Massachusetts was not yet solved. Second, it served to reinforce MADD's public image. All of these activities—the vigil, the CaringVan, the patient but persistent efforts to push for important legislation—were consistent with that image.

The stage was set for a major push on .08/.02. But then another bill moved to the fore in the closing days of the 1991 legislative session.

The Admissibility Bill

Under Massachusetts law, when a driver is arrested for alcohol-impaired driving, the driver is asked to take a breathalyzer test (breath test) to determine his or her blood alcohol content. The driver can refuse, but if he or she does, the driver loses his or her operator's license for 120 days. If the driver is prosecuted in court, however, the fact that he or she refused to take the breath test is *not* admissible as evidence.

MADD Massachusetts had long complained about this loophole in the law, which allowed repeat drunk drivers to evade criminal punishment by refusing to take the breath test. Ironically, this peculiarity of Massachusetts law was not widely known until a superior court judge was arrested for driving under the influence, declined to take the breath test, and then publicly explained the rationale for his decision.

Senate Bill 154 would have changed this law so that a driver's refusal to take a breath test could be admitted as evidence during trial. The measure had strong support from Governor Weld, Attorney General Scott Harshbarger, and every district attorney in the state. It had been filed every year since 1978 by Senator Paul D. Harold, a Democrat from Quincy, without success to that point.

Burke, the senator from Framingham, opposed this bill, claiming that the measure would violate a Massachusetts constitutional provision against self-incrimination. In fact, the U.S. Supreme Court had ruled in 1983 in *South Dakota v. Neville* that such a law did not violate the Fifth Amendment to the U.S. Constitution. When this was pointed out to the senator, he argued that the Massachusetts constitution provided even more stringent protections, which made the federal ruling moot.

This debate could have been easily resolved if the senate had requested the state's supreme judicial court to issue an advisory opinion, which is common practice in Massachusetts. According to state MADD officials, when there was a move to make such a request 2 years earlier, Burke had blocked it.

A second bill before the senate in late 1991 called for mandatory jail sentences for hit-and-run drivers who leave the scenes of crashes involving deaths or serious injuries. This measure was dubbed the "Heidi Wood Bill" in honor of a young girl who had been killed by such a driver. This measure was of intense concern to MADD since it was evident that alcohol-impaired drivers were leaving the scene so that they would have time to sober up.

In early December 1991, Burke moved to "table" both bills. Under the rules of the senate, any one senator can act to stall a piece of legislation for 30 days, and this can be done at any step of the legislative process. When a bill is tabled, no action of any kind can be taken on it. With the end of the session coming at the turn of the new year, Burke's action effectively killed both bills.

MADD Fights Back

MADD Massachusetts held a press conference just outside the senate chamber to bring attention to what Burke was doing. MADD's media alert carried the following headline: "MADD Vows to Fight Massachusetts Senator Ed Burke's 'One-Man Campaign' to Help Drunk Drivers Elude Punishment." The media alert articulated MADD's frustration, pointing out that by the rules of the senate, it is possible for a single senator to block the will of the majority.

At the press conference, MADD announced plans for volunteers to distribute 10,000 leaflets in Burke's district to inform voters about his repeated efforts to stall or kill new drunk driving legislation and to encourage them to call him, either at the senate or at home, to raise their voices in protest. MADD's patience was clearly at an end.

Two facts about Burke were emphasized during the press conference: that he is a defense attorney and that he has accepted alcohol political action committee (PAC) campaign contributions. Television news accounts focused on Heidi Wood's mother and sisters, who came to the press conference to show their support for the two bills that Burke was holding up. With the television cameras in mind, each family member wore a sweatshirt emblazoned with a full-color photograph of Heidi.

Bulger was visibly annoyed with MADD and the negative attention it was bringing to the senate. In one television news report, he was shown pushing his way past a crowd of MADD volunteers as he made his way to the senate chamber, refusing to offer any comment. Later that week, to demonstrate that its battle was with Burke and not the senate president, MADD sent Bulger 50 roses (1 for each of the 50 states) to thank him for his participation in the International Candlelight Vigil.

Burke relented. By the end of December 1991, the Heidi Wood Bill was signed into law to deal with hit-and-run drivers who leave the scene of serious crashes. Action on the admissibility bill was equally swift. The senate passed it 27–3. The house of representatives then passed it 144–0, and it was returned to the senate for engrossment, the formal rendering of the bill for the governor's signature.

To MADD's dismay, before the senate could take action to engross the admissibility bill, Burke tabled it for 30 days, which once again had the effect of killing the legislation. MADD and other traffic safety advocates lobbied the senate president to put pressure on Burke to back down, but to no avail.

Both major Boston newspapers wrote strong editorials urging that Senate Bill 154 be passed. The *Boston Herald* described Burke's maneuvering as a threat to public safety. *The Tab*, a chain of community-based newspapers, paired its editorial with an unflattering cartoon of Burke that ridiculed his opposition to the bill.

Burke still refused to give in. Allies in the senate and in the Weld administration told MADD Massachusetts that unless the organization took drastic action, the bill would die. Thus MADD again made the decision to go public with its unhappiness with Burke's actions.

MADD Fights Back: Round 2

MADD coordinated several media activities during the final week of the 1991 legislative session. First, MADD state chair Kay Dudley wrote an op-ed piece for the *Middlesex News*, which serves Burke's legislative district. Dudley closed by pointing out that Senate Bill 154 would "bring Massachusetts up to date with the rest of the country" since all but a handful of states have admissibility provisions.

Next, on the final day of the legislative session, MADD ran a paid advertisement on WBZ-AM to encourage supporters of the admissibility bill to call Burke's office to protest his actions. MADD called Burke's office to give the senator an opportunity to hear the ad before it ran so that he could reconsider his stance, but he refused the call. The 60-second ad ran twice that morning. It was hard-hitting and to the point:

> A driver's refusal to take a breathalyzer test cannot be admitted as evidence in a criminal trial for drunk driving.
>
> A defense attorney who defends habitual drunk drivers—that is, a defense attorney like Ed Burke—loves a loophole that makes his job easier. So a senator like Ed Burke will do anything he can to keep Senate Bill 154 from passing.
>
> Even though the state's district attorneys are clamoring for this loophole to be closed, and even though victims of drunk driving are pleading for 154, Senator Ed Burke doesn't care, and he's used every trick in the book to thwart the will of the majority.
>
> So, hail to Ed Burke, hero to drunk drivers and friend of the alcohol industry. Oh, yes. Did you know that Senator Burke takes PAC money from the alcohol industry?

Call Senator Burke of Framingham. Tell him to stop blocking
Senate Bill 154. If a drunk driver refuses to take a breath test,
the jury should know. Call [phone number].

Paid for by Mothers Against Drunk Driving.

The ad made deliberate use of symbols that would resonate with a
public that is concerned about the politicians who run its affairs such
as "defense attorney," "PAC money," and "conflict of interest."

The "main event" was a press conference at the state house to
announce that MADD was running the ad. Dudley explained MADD's
strategy as follows: "People have to know what this man is doing.
Senator Burke is out of touch with the voters in his district. The
people want safe roads." As Dudley spoke, a MADD volunteer held up
a sign with Burke's telephone number.

Television news coverage was extensive. Indeed, the confrontation
between MADD and Burke was the number one story that day. For a
group like MADD to take out an advertisement of this sort was
unprecedented in Massachusetts.

A MADD volunteer who visited the senator's office after the noon-
time news reports said the phone never stopped ringing as person
after person called in to express outrage over his actions. Some of the
callers were MADD members who had been alerted in advance. In the
end, Burke did not back down, but no one had expected him to do so.

The following day, state house reporter Frank Phillips of the *Boston
Globe* wrote that sources had told him that MADD's tactics against
Burke "undermined efforts to persuade him to drop his opposition.
Several senate colleagues said Burke had seemed to be softening in his
position, but dug in after the attacks."

Burke tried to put his own spin on events. He denied MADD's con-
flict-of-interest charges, claiming that in his career he had represented
only a handful of drunk driving clients and that he was unaware of
accepting PAC money from the alcohol industry. Burke expressed
regret over what he called MADD's "guerrilla pressure tactics," saying
that the organization had demeaned itself.

If it was true that Burke had been rethinking his position, no one
had bothered to tell MADD representatives or Senator Harold, the bill's
sponsor. MADD Massachusetts dismissed the *Boston Globe* story as an
effort by the senate leadership to silence MADD and other citizen
groups. "In fact, we had nothing to lose," Dudley said in an interview.

Examining MADD's Media Strategy

Despite the bill's failure in 1991, MADD's media advocacy strategy did
serve its purposes. First, MADD's hardball tactics demonstrated that
the organization had political clout. To MADD's surprise, Burke
announced in mid-January 1992 that he would not run for reelection
later that year.

Second, the issue no longer was whether Senate Bill 154 was constitutional; rather, it was the fact that a single senator could prevent the legislative process from working. The Massachusetts senate operates by arcane rules that can violate the public interest, and MADD brought new attention to that fact.

Third, the controversy led the *Boston Globe*, the *Boston Herald*, and other newspapers to go on record in support of the bill. The news media continued to take a deep interest in the admissibility bill and followed it closely as the new legislative year commenced.

The whole mess had made the senate look bad, and Senate President Bulger was motivated to remedy that by pushing for quick action on the bill in 1992. Bulger promised MADD that the bill would be "fast-tracked" in 1992 so that if anyone tabled the bill, it would happen early enough in the legislative session to prevent the bill from being killed.

Bulger made good on his promise. In early February 1992, the senate asked the supreme judicial court for an advisory opinion on the bill (now Senate Bill 717). Burke maintained that even if the court ruled the bill to be constitutional, he would still oppose it.

The court rendered its advisory opinion 3 months later, stating that the law would violate the Massachusetts constitution's provision against self-incrimination. In essence, the court declared that Burke was right. Burke was elated. "[This shows] the need to stick to your guns when you think a serious constitutional issue is involved, even though there is a lot of public political support," the senator said.

The Aftermath for MADD Massachusetts

MADD Massachusetts' decision to confront Burke was sharply criticized by some rank-and-file members of the organization, who first learned of the state office's actions by watching the television news. All of the local chapter leaders had been given a chance to comment on the ad before it aired, but after MADD's feud with Burke hit the airwaves, some began to have second thoughts and became sharply critical of Dudley and the other MADD volunteers who had planned the media advocacy effort.

Burke himself launched a public relations campaign to redeem his reputation. As part of that effort, he portrayed MADD as a group of zealots. In early 1992, the *Boston Globe Magazine* helped the senator's cause by quoting him at length about his battle with MADD in an article on victims' rights groups titled "Revenging Angels."

As the supreme judicial court considered its opinion on the admissibility bill in early 1992, internal dissension within MADD Massachusetts continued to fester. MADD's good name had been sullied, several chapter leaders now complained. The MADD chapter leader from Burke's district was especially vocal in criticizing what he called a "personal attack" on Burke. The whole affair was "unseemly," he said.

Another chapter leader even questioned why MADD was involved in promoting legislation.

For some chapter leaders, the "hardball" tactics used against Burke reinforced their apprehensions about the Massachusetts state office. During the late 1980s, MADD National had started to demand greater fiscal accountability from its 400-plus local chapters and had enlisted the help of the various state offices to enforce its tighter rules. Because the state offices had no line authority over the chapters, their intrusion into chapter affairs created widespread, although not universal, resentment.

But there was still another factor at work in Massachusetts. News reporters who once had turned to the chapter heads for quotes and on-camera appearances now turned instead to Dudley, the state chairperson. Unfortunately, some local leaders found it difficult to accept the change.

Under MADD's rules, the state chairperson served at the pleasure of a state committee made up of local chapter leaders. As the internecine battles grew more heated, fueled by the Burke controversy, Dudley eventually decided not to run for another term as chair of the state organization.

A few months later, Dudley offered to continue serving MADD as its chief liaison with the state house. Her offer was spurned even though she was well known and widely respected among the legislators, two governors of different political parties each had appointed her to serve on a judicial nominating committee, and there was no one else available from MADD who could volunteer the kind of time she had available.

As a result, MADD Massachusetts lost its most effective voice for policy change and MADD's efforts to push for .08/.02 became stalled.

Looking Back

Clearly, the media advocacy strategies used to publicize Burke's maneuvering brought MADD's internal problems in Massachusetts to a flash point. Was the state office unwise in moving forward without first building a firmer consensus among the local chapter leaders? With hindsight, it is easy to draw that conclusion.

On the other hand, given the previous antagonism between the state office and the chapters, it is not clear whether a strong united front, one that would remain intact in the face of outside attack, was really possible. For the right issue, it might have been worth it for the state office to pursue this kind of aggressive media advocacy strategy despite the internal costs to MADD. The admissibility bill was not the right issue.

The most important lesson from this cautionary tale is this: Leaders of volunteer organizations who want to work for policy change must proceed cautiously before deciding what type of media advocacy strategy to use or even whether to use the media at all.

Prior to launching a media advocacy effort, the organization's capacity for planning and executing such an effort must be realistically appraised. Is there a strong volunteer base with the required knowledge and expertise? Does the press see the organization as a legitimate source of accurate information? Does the public hold the organization in high regard? Are there financial resources for paid radio advertising or staging press events? Is there an articulate spokesperson who knows how to work effectively with the news media? MADD Massachusetts had all of this in place in late 1991.

The organization's leaders must also take a hard look at themselves to determine whether they can withstand the pressures that might result when a media advocacy strategy is used. This means that the leaders must be united in supporting this approach, even with the controversy it might bring. There must be a spirit of goodwill and trust among them, which may be tested if strong political forces act in opposition to the organization. Unfortunately, Massachusetts MADD, with the long-simmering problems between the state office and the local chapters, did not present a united front.

Finally, the organization's leaders must identify their key policy objectives and then stick to that agenda. An organization such as MADD, with its strong volunteer base and a noble cause, has solid political capital, but that capital can be quickly exhausted. This means that MADD, like any group that has been organized for a political purpose, must spend its political capital wisely. In the case of the admissibility bill, that did not occur. Burke's parliamentary gamesmanship so infuriated MADD volunteers that they lost sight of their more important, long-term objectives.

From a prevention standpoint, with the need for a strategy of general deterrence firmly in view, the admissibility bill was of minor importance. Even without the law, a Massachusetts driver who refuses to take a breath test can still lose his or her license for 120 days, the kind of immediate penalty that is known to have a deterrent effect. Of greater importance for reducing alcohol-related traffic fatalities was MADD's proposal to lower the BAC limit, which evaluation studies have shown will save many lives. Two years elapsed before the Massachusetts legislature again gave serious consideration to that proposal.

CHAPTER 4

LEGAL ISSUES CONCERNING DRUNK DRIVING

THE EFFECTIVENESS OF BLOOD ALCOHOL CONCENTRATION LAWS

General Accounting Office

Many states have passed laws making it illegal to drive if one's blood alcohol concentration (BAC) is above a certain amount. A number of states have set this limit as low as .08 BAC, but the effectiveness of this low level is a matter of debate. The following selection is excerpted from a report prepared by the General Accounting Office (GAO), which evaluates the cost-effectiveness of federal government programs. The GAO's report focuses on three studies sponsored by the National Highway Traffic Safety Administration (NHTSA) that examined the effectiveness of .08 BAC laws. Examining the studies, the GAO states that some showed evidence that the implementation of .08 BAC laws corresponded with a decrease in alcohol-related fatalities, but none of the studies conclusively proved that the .08 BAC laws were the sole cause of the reduction of fatal crashes. However, the GAO maintains that .08 laws can be an important part of a program of countermeasures that together can combat traffic fatalities that result from drunk driving.

Since 1970, the National Highway Traffic Safety Administration (NHTSA) has espoused a "systems approach" to reducing drunk driving, including enforcement, judicial, legislative, licensing, and public information components. In 1997, NHTSA published an action plan developed with other participants to reduce alcohol-related driving fatalities to 11,000 by the year 2005. This plan recommended that all states pass a wide range of laws, including ones establishing .08 blood alcohol concentration (BAC) limits, license revocation laws—under which a person deemed to be driving under the influence has his or her driving privileges suspended or revoked—comprehensive screening and treatment programs for alcohol offenders, vehicle impoundment, "zero tolerance" BAC and other laws for youth, and primary enforcement laws for safety belts. The plan also called for increased public awareness campaigns, with an emphasis on target populations

Excerpted from "Highway Safety: Effectiveness of State .08 Blood Alcohol Laws," a publication of the U.S. General Accounting Office, Washington, D.C.

such as young people and repeat offenders.

The value of public education and enforcement has been demonstrated in a number of studies. A NHTSA evaluation of a sobriety checkpoint program in Tennessee, a state with a .10 BAC limit, concluded that the program and its attendant publicity reduced alcohol-related fatal accidents in that state by 20.4%.

The Principal Arguments

One of NHTSA's principal arguments for nationwide adoption of .08 BAC laws is that the medical evidence of drivers' impairment at that level is substantial and conclusive. According to NHTSA, reaction time, tracking and steering, and emergency responses are impaired at even low levels, and substantially impaired at .08 BAC. As a result, the risk of being in a motor vehicle crash increases when alcohol is involved, and increases dramatically at .08 BAC and higher levels. In contrast to NHTSA's position, industry associations critical of .08 BAC laws contend that .08 BAC is an acceptable level of impairment for driving a motor vehicle and that these laws penalize "responsible social drinking."

These associations also believe that .08 BAC laws do not address the problem of drunk driving because many more drivers using alcohol are reported at the "high" BAC levels (above .10 BAC) than at the lower BAC levels. Because we were directed to review the impact of .08 BAC laws on the number and severity of crashes involving alcohol, we did not review the medical evidence on impairment or other arguments in favor of or in opposition to .08 BAC laws.

NHTSA also believes that lowering the BAC limit to .08 is a proven effective measure that will reduce the number of crashes and save lives. For example, in a December 1997 publication, NHTSA stated that "recent research . . . has been quite conclusive in showing the impaired driving reductions already attributable to .08, as well as the potential for saving additional lives if all states adopted .08 BAC laws." In May 1998, the NHTSA Administrator stated, "The traffic safety administration is aware of four published studies, . . . [and] each study has shown that lowering the illegal blood alcohol limit to .08 is associated with significant reductions in alcohol-related fatal crashes." In a fact sheet distributed to state legislatures considering these laws, NHTSA stated that the agency's "analysis of five states that lowered the BAC limit to .08 showed that significant decreases in alcohol-related fatal crashes occurred in four out of the five states as a result of the legislation." NHTSA used these study results to encourage states to enact .08 BAC laws, testifying in one instance before a state legislature: "We conservatively project a 10% reduction in alcohol-related crashes, deaths, and injuries" in the state.

Seven studies have been published assessing the effect of .08 BAC laws on motor vehicle crashes and fatalities in the United States. Four studies published between 1991 and 1996 assessed the effectiveness of .08 BAC laws in the five states that enacted them between 1983 and 1991. On April 28, 1999, NHTSA released three additional studies.

Although NHTSA characterized the first four studies on the effectiveness of .08 BAC laws as conclusively establishing that .08 BAC laws resulted in substantial reductions in fatalities involving alcohol, we found that three of the four studies had limitations and raised methodological concerns that called their conclusions into question. For example, while a NHTSA-endorsed Boston University study concluded that 500 to 600 fewer fatal crashes would occur each year if all states adopted .08 BAC laws, this study has been criticized for, among other reasons, its method of comparing states; and a recent NHTSA study characterized the earlier study's conclusion as "unwarranted." The fourth study reported mixed results. Therefore, these studies did not provide conclusive evidence that .08 BAC laws by themselves have resulted in reductions in drunk driving crashes and fatalities. A task force of the New Jersey State Senate examined this evidence and, in a report issued in December 1998, reached a similar conclusion.

On April 28, 1999, NHTSA released three studies that it sponsored. These studies are more comprehensive than the earlier studies and show many positive results but fall short of conclusively establishing that .08 BAC laws by themselves have resulted in reductions in alcohol-related fatalities. For example, during the early 1990s, when the involvement of alcohol in traffic fatalities declined from around 50% to nearly 40%—a trend in states with both .08 BAC and .10 BAC laws—eight states' .08 BAC laws became effective, and the recent studies disagree on the degree to which .08 BAC laws played a role. Two of the studies reached different conclusions about the effect of one state's .08 BAC law; one concluded that the law brought about reductions in drunk driving deaths in North Carolina, while another concluded that the state's reductions occurred as the result of a long-term trend that began before the law was enacted.

In a statement releasing the three studies, NHTSA credited the nation's progress in reducing drunk driving to a combination of strict state laws and tougher enforcement, and stated that "these three studies provide additional support for the premise that .08 BAC laws help to reduce alcohol-related fatalities, particularly when they are implemented in conjunction with other impaired driving laws and programs."

The 11-State Study

An April 1999 NHTSA study of 11 states with .08 BAC laws assessed whether the states experienced statistically significant reductions in three measures of alcohol involvement in crashes after the law took effect: (1) the number of fatalities in crashes in which any alcohol was involved, (2) the number of fatalities in crashes where drivers had a BAC of .10 or greater ("high BAC"), and (3) the proportion of fatalities involving "high BAC" drivers to fatalities involving sober drivers. The study performed a similar analysis for license revocation laws and also modeled and controlled for any pre-existing long-term declining trends these states may have been experiencing when their .08 BAC laws went into effect. The study found that five of the 11 states had reductions in at least one measure and that two of the 11 states had reductions in all three measures.

The study was careful not to draw a causal relationship between the reductions it found and the passage of .08 BAC laws by themselves. Rather, it concluded that .08 BAC laws added to the impact that enforcement, public information, and legislative activities, particularly license revocation laws, were having. In addition to the two states where .08 BAC and license revocation laws were found to be effective in combination, the study noted that the five states with .08 BAC laws that showed reductions already had license revocation laws in place. One of the authors told us that this suggested the .08 BAC laws had the effect of expanding the scope of the license revocation laws to a new portion of the driving public.

The University of North Carolina Study

A NHTSA-sponsored study by the University of North Carolina concluded, in contrast to the 11-state study, that the .08 BAC law in North Carolina had little clear effect. The study examined alcohol-related crashes and crashes involving drivers with BACs greater than .10 from 1991 through 1995; compared fatalities among drivers with BACs greater than .10 in North Carolina with such fatalities in 11 other states; and compared six measures of alcohol involvement in North Carolina and 37 states that did not have .08 BAC laws at that time. The study controlled for and commented on external factors that could confound the results, such as the state's sobriety checkpoints, enforcement, and media coverage. The study found the following:

• No statistically significant decrease in alcohol-related crashes after passage of North Carolina's .08 BAC law in three direct and two "proxy" measures.

• A continual decline in the proportion of fatally injured drivers with BACs equal to or greater than .10 but no abrupt change in fatalities that could be attributed to the .08 BAC law.

• Decreases in alcohol-related crashes in North Carolina and in the 11 other states studied. While North Carolina's decreases were greater, the study concluded that no specific effects could be attributed to the .08 BAC law.

• No statistically significant difference between North Carolina and 37 states without .08 BAC laws in four of the six measures. While reductions in police-reported and estimated instances of alcohol involvement were found to be statistically significant, these reductions happened 18 months before North Carolina lowered its BAC limit. The authors attributed these decreases, in part, to increased enforcement.

The study concluded that the .08 BAC law had little clear effect on alcohol-related fatalities in North Carolina, that a downward trend was already occurring before North Carolina enacted its .08 BAC law, and that this trend was not affected by the law. The authors offered several possible explanations, including (1) the effects of the .08 BAC laws were obscured by a broader change in drinking-driving behavior that was already occurring; (2) North Carolina had made substantial progress combating drunk driving and that the remaining drinking and driving population in North Carolina was simply not responsive to the lower BAC law; and (3) .08 BAC laws are not effective in measurably affecting the behavior of drinking drivers.

The 50-State Study

The third April 1999 NHTSA study evaluated .08 BAC laws by comparing two groups—states with .08 BAC laws with states with .10 BAC laws, before and after the laws were passed. This study concluded that states that enacted .08 BAC laws experienced an 8% reduction in the involvement of drivers with both high and low BACs when compared with the involvement of sober drivers. The study estimated that 274 lives have been saved in the states that enacted .08 BAC laws and that 590 lives could be saved annually if all states enacted .08 BAC laws.

While more comprehensive than other studies, the study used a method to calculate the 8% reduction that is different from, and thus not directly comparable to, those for fatality estimates reported in other studies and publications. In particular, this method can produce a numerical effect that is larger than other methods.

Another reason why this study's results cannot be directly compared to other studies' is because it did not include data for drivers under 21. In 1997, drivers under 21 accounted for around 14% of the drivers in fatal crashes and about 12% of the drivers in fatal crashes involving alcohol.

Including persons under 21 years old would have changed these study results. In particular, the study would have found no statistically significant reductions associated with .08 BAC laws for drivers at low BAC levels. The findings regarding drivers at high BAC levels—a group that contains over three times as many drivers—would have remained substantially unchanged.

The study warns that "it is important to interpret estimates of lives saved due to any single law with considerable caution." In particular, as the study notes, factors such as public education, enforcement, and changes in societal norms and attitudes toward alcohol have produced long-term reductions in drunk driving deaths over many years. This study did more to control for extraneous factors than any of the other multi-state studies, but this is inherently difficult to do, and in this case the authors estimate that 50% to 60% of the reductions in alcohol-related fatalities are explained by the laws it reviewed and the other factors it considered, a moderate level for statistical analyses of this type. Because of the uncertainties, the study's estimate of lives saved is also expressed as a range—and the number of lives saved in states with .08 BAC laws could have been as few as 88 or as many as 472.

While the study reported results for the three laws it reviewed, including .08 BAC laws, the study also concluded that "the attribution of savings to any single law should be made with caution since each new law builds to some extent on existing legislation and on other ongoing trends and activities."

Inconclusive Results

While indications are that .08 BAC laws in combination with other drunk driving laws, as well as sustained public education and information efforts and strong enforcement, can be effective, the evidence does not conclusively establish that .08 BAC laws by themselves result in reductions in the number and severity of crashes involving alcohol. Until 1991, limited published evidence existed on the effectiveness of .08 BAC laws, and NHTSA's position—that this evidence was conclusive—was overstated. In 1999, more comprehensive studies have been published that show many positive results, and NHTSA's characterization of the results has been more balanced. Nevertheless, these studies fall short of providing conclusive evidence that .08 BAC laws by themselves have been responsible for reductions in fatal crashes.

Because a state enacting a .08 BAC law may or may not see a decline in alcohol-related fatalities, it is difficult to predict accurately how many lives would be saved if all states passed .08 BAC laws. The effect of a .08 BAC law depends on a number of factors, including the degree to which the law is publicized; how well it is enforced; other drunk driving laws in effect; and the unique culture of each state, particularly public attitudes concerning alcohol.

As drunk driving continues to claim the lives of thousands of Americans each year, governments at all levels seek solutions. Many states are considering enacting .08 BAC laws, and the Congress is considering requiring all states to enact these laws. Although a strong causal link between .08 BAC laws by themselves and reductions in traffic fatalities is absent, other evidence, including medical evidence on impairment, should be considered when evaluating the effectiveness of .08 BAC laws. A .08 BAC law can be an important component of a state's overall highway safety program, but a .08 BAC law alone is not a "silver bullet." Highway safety research shows that the best countermeasure against drunk driving is a combination of laws, sustained public education, and vigorous enforcement.

THE PROS AND CONS OF LOWER BLOOD ALCOHOL CONCENTRATION LAWS

Paul F. Rothberg

A number of states have passed laws making it illegal to drive with a blood alcohol concentration (BAC) higher than .08, and supporters of these laws want the .08 BAC limit to be implemented nationwide. In the following report, prepared for the U.S. Congress by the Congressional Research Service, Paul F. Rothberg examines the research concerning .08 BAC laws and presents the arguments for and against lowering BAC laws to .08. According to Rothberg, advocates argue that a .08 BAC limit would save lives, serve as a deterrent to drinking and driving, and encourage law enforcement personnel to arrest and convict drunk drivers. On the other hand, the author notes, opponents claim that most drunk drivers who cause fatal crashes have a BAC much higher than .08. They maintain that other countermeasures are sufficient to reduce fatalities due to drunk driving, he writes. Rothberg works for the Science Policy Research Division of the Congressional Research Service.

As of March 1998, in all but two states, it is illegal per se (by definition) to operate a motor vehicle with a blood alcohol concentration (BAC) at or above a specified amount. In the 48 states with a per se law, impairment does not have to be proven, but rather, evidence of alcohol at or above a specified BAC level is one of the factors needed to convict someone of either driving under the influence (DUI) or driving while intoxicated (DWI), depending on the state involved. In 33 states and the District of Columbia this amount is set at 0.10 BAC for all drivers aged 21 and above. As of March 1998, 15 states have enacted a 0.08 BAC law.

As part of the debate over reauthorization of the various federal surface transportation programs, an amendment to require each state either to enact a 0.08 BAC law or face the loss of a certain percentage of its Federal Highway Trust Fund monies passed the Senate and will

Excerpted from "Drunk Driving: Should Each State Be Required to Enact a 0.08 Blood Alcohol Concentration (BAC) Law?" by Paul F. Rothberg, a report dated March 27, 1998, from the Congressional Research Service of the Library of Congress. Endnotes in the original have been omitted in this reprint.

likely be considered in the House. [Editor's note: The amendment was removed before the bill passed in the House in May 1998. President Bill Clinton signed the bill in June 1998.] This proposal raises questions about the effectiveness and impacts of a 0.08 BAC law, the rights of states versus the federal government, and alternative ways to encourage the states to adopt stronger impaired driving countermeasures. This report first summarizes key studies that quantify the impacts of a 0.08 BAC law. Then, selected arguments are presented in favor and against a 0.08 BAC law or the imposition of a penalty against any state that does not enact such a measure.

Examining the Effects of Blood Alcohol Concentration

In 1996, 41 percent of some 42,000 deaths due to traffic crashes were alcohol-related. According to the National Highway Traffic Safety Administration (NHTSA), 82 percent of the drinking drivers involved in these crashes had a BAC level exceeding 0.08 percent. The Insurance Institute for Highway Safety asserts that the relative risk of being killed in a single vehicle crash with a driver operating at a BAC between .05 and .09 percent is at least 9 times higher than that of a driver who had not consumed any alcohol. Crash risk increases as BAC level increases.

To reach the 0.08 BAC level, an average male weighing 170 pounds must consume more than four drinks within one hour on an empty stomach. At the 0.08 BAC level, braking, steering, lane changing, and judgement are degraded and virtually all drivers are substantially impaired.

Numerous investigators have analyzed how different measures of driver-related performance are reduced at different blood alcohol levels. These studies typically compare performance on a specific task related to driving at different BACs against a baseline measure of performance of no alcohol. These studies suggest a decrement range (from the control baselines) of roughly 10 percent to 70 percent, with the median at about 35 percent, for a 0.08 BAC level. In reviewing the literature, NHTSA concluded that a general pattern appears showing a decrease in performance of a particular task at the lowest BAC level and a further decrease in performance with increases in BAC.

Reviewing the Research

To what extent does a 0.08 BAC law help save lives? There are only a few studies that provide a quantitative answer to this question. Four key studies reported in the literature use different measures or methodologies to determine the relative success or impact of a 0.08 BAC law. For example in a study which compared five states with a 0.08 BAC law to five similar or control states that had not enacted this statute but had a 0.10 BAC law, investigators found that, overall, states with 0.08 BAC laws experienced a post-law reduction of 16 percent in the proportion of fatal crashes involving fatally-injured drivers whose BAC was 0.08 percent or greater. Because states vary on many different factors, it is difficult to pick ideal control states for comparison purposes. When different control states are used, different results may be reached. Another study analyzed six different measures of driver involvement in alcohol-related fatal crashes in each of five states before and after the effective date of a 0.08 BAC law. The study revealed statistically significant reductions in 9 out of 30 data points (6 measures in each of 5 states) of driver involvement once a 0.08 BAC law became effective.

It, however, is difficult to quantify precisely the effect that is attributable only to a state reducing its per se law from 0.10 BAC to 0.08 BAC. The impacts of changes in other state traffic laws or increased police enforcement in a particular state are two examples of spurious or confounding variables that could affect research results. Two other studies reported in the literature deal only with the impacts of a 0.08 BAC law on one state and are therefore excluded from this analysis because of problems generalizing from these studies and other limitations, such as the introduction of administrative license revocation shortly after the introduction of 0.08 BAC law in this same state.

Balancing the Benefits and Costs

The potential benefits of 0.08 BAC laws need to be considered within the context of potential costs. This analysis is difficult because there are relatively few studies that quantify these costs. Nevertheless, it is well known that arrest of alcohol-impaired drivers is a high priority in the law enforcement community and it is considered a fundamental and necessary cost. To the extent that the reduction in a BAC limit from 0.10 to 0.08 percent leads to more arrests, additional demands are placed on enforcement resources and time. With recent reductions in traffic enforcement resources in many states, the time needed to enforce effectively 0.08 BAC laws only compounds resource problems. But the incremental costs of processing additional violators due to enforcement of a 0.08 BAC law, instead of a 0.10 BAC law, are relatively minor, especially when considered within the framework of total law enforcement costs. Thus, the incremental costs of implementing a 0.08 BAC law instead of a 0.10 BAC law appear to be minimal.

On the other hand, the potential costs savings to society that might be realized as a result of implementation of a 0.08 BAC law are quite large. The benefits accrued from one or two lives saved every few years in any one jurisdiction would more than pay for the additional costs of additional arrests due to enforcing a 0.08 BAC law. Furthermore, there are other savings for enforcement personnel when their states enact a 0.08 law. As a NHTSA study found, "The major difference is that, in cases where the chemical test indicates a BAC of 0.08 or 0.09, it is no longer necessary for the arresting officer to produce supporting evidence demonstrating the individual is under the influence." This same study found that the reduction in the BAC limit from 0.10 percent to 0.08 percent had minimal impacts on the way court administrators and judges implement their responsibilities.

If decision makers in state governments are to make more informed choices on whether to enact 0.08 BAC laws, then additional evaluation studies are needed. Future studies could examine the impacts of this measure over a longer period of time and in additional states. Until additional evidence is developed that makes a more compelling case, the reliability of estimates forecasting the potential number of alcohol-involved fatal crashes that might be prevented as a result of nationwide enactment of 0.08 BAC laws is uncertain. The NHTSA does have underway a variety of additional studies examining the impacts of 0.08 BAC laws. Additional research on the costs of implementing 0.08 BAC laws on the law enforcement community and the court system also would assist decision makers.

The Advocates

Numerous health, safety, law enforcement and insurance groups favor enactment of a 0.08 BAC law in each state; but there are substantial disagreements as to how this goal is to be achieved. For example, Mothers Against Drunk Driving and Advocates for Highway and Auto Safety favor the imposition of a penalty against any state failing to enact a 0.08 BAC law. The U.S. Department of Transportation (DOT) now supports the imposition of a penalty against those states that fail to enact a 0.08 BAC law. In contrast, the National Association of Governors' Highway Safety Representatives favors each state enacting a 0.08 BAC per se law, but is against imposition of a penalty.

Advocates of 0.08 BAC laws present many different arguments in favor of enactment of this measure, including:

- The 0.08 BAC level is the appropriate and scientifically- based legal definition for a conviction aimed at combating impaired driving. This per se level recognizes that at 0.08 BAC all motorists are too impaired to drive safely.
- Vigorous implementation of 0.08 BAC laws serves as a general deterrent to people drinking and then driving, and thus helps prevent crashes due to alcohol use. In those states with a 0.08 BAC law, potential drivers who have been drinking may ask themselves: Will my next drink push me over the legal limit? Am I willing to risk an arrest and likely conviction for drunk driving?
- Reducing the blood alcohol level needed for a conviction of DWI or DUI from 0.10 BAC to 0.08 BAC may reduce the likelihood that a prosecutor will plea bargain for a lesser charge when someone tests near the 0.10 BAC level. In other words, a prosecutor might be more inclined to seek conviction of a seriously impaired driver whose BAC limit is marginally at the 0.10 level

under a 0.08 BAC statute than under a 0.10 BAC statute. Under a 0.10 BAC law, some prosecutors might be more inclined to plea bargain if someone tests slightly above or at 0.10 BAC.

- The 0.08 BAC level will increase the willingness of some law enforcement personnel to spend the time and resources necessary first to arrest someone for driving under the influence or while intoxicated, and then to participate in court proceedings by supplying documentation needed for a conviction.

- Effective implementation of a 0.08 BAC law has the potential for preventing as many as 500 to 600 fatal crashes each year due to alcohol. This calculation assumes a 5 percent reduction in alcohol-related fatalities in those states with 0.10 BAC laws in 1996.

The Penalty

Those who support a provision that would require any state that does not have a 0.08 BAC law to lose a portion of its Federal Highway Trust Fund monies argue:

- Experience demonstrates that the threat of losing highway trust fund monies gets the attention of state legislatures and stimulates the approval of stronger traffic safety laws. This approach has proven useful in convincing all states to adopt age 21 drinking laws and in convincing 47 states to adopt zero tolerance laws for drivers less than 21 years old.

- It is in the national interest to convince all of the states to enact 0.08 BAC statutes. This objective will only be accomplished in a timely manner if the federal government threatens to reduce the highway trust fund monies of a state.

The Opponents

Those who are against 0.08 BAC laws could argue:

- There are relatively few drivers (850–1000) estimated to have a 0.08 to 0.10 BAC who are involved in fatal crashes each year. Most of the alcohol-related fatal crashes involve drinking drivers operating at 0.10 BAC or above. New laws should focus on the problem driver impaired with a substantial quantity of alcohol, perhaps at 0.14 BAC or higher.

- There are many other countermeasures, such as administrative license revocation and sobriety road checks, that have been shown to be effective in reducing fatalities resulting from alcohol-impaired driving. During the last 15 years, there has been a steady decline in alcohol-related traffic deaths, even without widespread implementation of 0.08 BAC laws.

- A 0.08 BAC law could adversely affect the alcohol and restaurant industries by reducing the amount of alcohol consumed. Some maintain that a 0.08 BAC would adversely affect those who want to drink socially.

Debate over enactment of a 0.08 BAC law raises the question: At what blood alcohol level should it be illegal to operate a vehicle? Different levels have been imposed on different types of drivers and different age groups. For example, for younger drivers, 47 states have decided this level is 0.02 BAC or less. A truck or bus driver that is convicted of operating a commercial vehicle at or above the 0.04 BAC level is disqualified for at least one year according to federal and state regulations. Even though a 0.08 BAC level for non-commercial drivers of age 21 or older would bring this nation closer to the impaired driving limit now used by many other industrialized countries, most states have chosen to use the 0.10 BAC cutoff.

The imposition of a federal penalty would raise an array of additional concerns. Many state officials and organizations, such as the National Conference of State Legislatures, assert that each state should determine its own traffic safety laws without federal pressure or dictates. Since 1990 roughly two states each year have enacted a 0.08 BAC law, without the threat of a federally-imposed sanction. Many other states are considering the enactment of such a measure. In addition, those against the proposed penalty could assert that this sanction would be contrary to a current shift of power away from the federal government to the states. Others also could argue that the weight of evidence documenting the effectiveness of a 0.08 BAC law needs to be strengthened before the federal government forces enactment of this measure on all states.

Considering Other Options

There are other options that might be considered to encourage the adoption of 0.08 BAC laws as well as other alcohol countermeasures. Congress could reauthorize the basic concept embodied in the existing alcohol countermeasure program called the Section 410 program. This traffic safety incentive grant program provides the states with additional monies from the Federal Highway Trust Fund (above their apportioned amount) if a state enacts or implements a variety of traffic safety countermeasures aimed at reducing alcohol- impaired driving. Both the House and Senate reauthorization initiatives propose such incentives.

During the last 15 or so years, several different federal penalties threatened against the highway apportionment of a state have been imposed with mixed results. The use of such sanctions to achieve national purposes typically raises objections from the states. As stated by the National Association of Governors' Highway Safety Representatives:

> Sanctions also ignore the efforts of the states to do the right thing. Currently 20 states' legislatures are considering 0.08 BAC legislation. If any of the states fail at these efforts, they could be penalized, regardless of how hard they tried to enact

the necessary legislation. Sanctions create a tremendous amount of state resentment toward the federal government, even if the sanctions are for good public policy purposes. Repeated use of penalties and sanctions do much to reinforce negative state attitudes toward safety issues—exactly the opposite of what the federal government intends.

It also can be argued that sanctions should be reserved for only those traffic safety initiatives that would save the largest number of lives. For example, if all states adopted primary seat belt enforcement laws, the potential life savings would probably be substantially larger than if all states adapted a 0.08 BAC.

Debate over such initiatives as a 0.08 BAC per se limit which seek to strengthen state laws regarding impaired driving due to alcohol use evoke substantial emotions. The imposition of a penalty against a state for not enacting a 0.08 BAC statute would add to the intensity of the ongoing debate, but would most likely accelerate the adoption rate of this measure. Even without a sanction, additional states will likely adopt this measure, but at a slower pace. The multiple facets of this issue suggest that the current debate over 0.08 BAC laws, with or without a federal sanction provision, is likely to continue at either the federal or state levels for several years.

Pressuring Lawmakers: The Mothers Against Drunk Driving Lobby

Eric Peters

According to syndicated columnist Eric Peters, sometimes the acts of well-intentioned lobbying groups serve only to justify their existence. In particular, he cites Mothers Against Drunk Driving (MADD), which is pressuring lawmakers to force states to lower the permissible blood alcohol concentration (BAC) for drivers to .08. Peters reveals evidence that MADD, with the support of the National Highway Traffic Safety Administration (NHTSA), has mis-led lawmakers into believing that .08 BAC laws will reduce fatalities. However, according to the author, other studies have found that .08 BAC laws do not significantly reduce fatality rates but instead simply increase the number of people—mostly harmless social drinkers—arrested for drunk driving. The ensuing increase in drunk driving arrests, Peters claims, would create the continued need for organizations such as MADD. He concludes that in this particular case, MADD's actions and motives are suspect.

Mothers Against Drunk Driving (MADD) was founded in 1980 by Candy Lightner after a drunken man who had multiple convictions for driving while intoxicated ran down and killed her 13-year-old daughter. MADD quickly helped make drunk driving one of the most heavily combatted social scourges in the nation. But now the group has embarked on a crusade that has even former adherents wondering whether it has gone too far.

Putting Pressure on the States

Mrs. Lightner herself has quit MADD because she thinks it has become "overzealous." The group is now devoting its energies to putting pressure on state legislatures around the country to lower the permissible Blood Alcohol Content for drivers from .10 to .08. Such a change would not increase safety on the roads, but it would increase the number of supposedly "drunk" drivers—and, hence, the perceived

Reprinted, with permission, from "MADD House," by Eric Peters, *National Review*, September 28, 1998; © 1998 by National Review, Inc., www.nationalreview.com.

need for MADD. It is a typical story of a well-intentioned lobbying group becoming a self-perpetuating Washington institution.

MADD argues that even "at .08 BAC, a driver is 16 times more likely to be involved in a crash" than if he had consumed no alcohol at all. MADD President Karolyn Nunnallee contends that "many people are dangerously impaired at even .05 BAC" (about the level most people would have after one beer on an empty stomach). In the spring of 1998, MADD sought to have Congress force the .08 standard on all the states—sixteen already have it—by incorporating language into the Transportation Bill that would have tied distribution of federal highway dollars to adoption of .08 BAC. The provision was killed at the last minute.

Should it have been? Dr. H. Laurence Ross, a professor at the University of New Mexico and author of *Confronting Drunk Driving*, points out that "the potential of alcohol to impair drivers and cause accidents is directly proportionate to the amount consumed." According to Dr. Ross, adoption of the .08 standard has the potential to increase by 60 per cent the number of motorists arrested for "drunk driving"—but without any concomitant decrease in either fatality or accident rates.

Accident statistics show that impairment of driving ability seldom takes place until BAC levels exceed .10. A BAC of .08 or less means there is little enough alcohol in his or her system that it is extremely unlikely to appreciably affect coordination, reaction times, vision, or judgment in a normal person. The man who killed Candy Lightner's daughter had a BAC of .20—and most of the weaving drunks pulled over by cops have BAC levels above .10.

The evidence confirms this at every turn:

- In 1996, more than 62 per cent of all traffic fatalities considered to be "alcohol-related" were the work of drivers with BAC levels above .14—almost twice the .08 level.
- According to the National Highway Traffic Safety Administration (NHTSA), fatality rates don't go up appreciably until you get above .10 BAC.
- A study by the Harvard Injury Control Center found that 67 per cent of those drivers who were killed in automobile accidents after drinking had BAC levels of .15 or higher.
- Fewer deaths occur in accidents involving drivers with BACs between .08 and .09 than involving those with BACs between .01 and .03, which is cough-syrup territory.

Misleading the Lawmakers

"MADD's number-one priority is to lower the arrest threshold for DWI to .08—even though this level makes it illegal for a 120-pound woman to drive after consuming just two glasses of wine over the course of two hours," says Rick Berman of the Alcohol Beverage Institute, the lobbying arm of the liquor industry, which played a critical role in stripping the .08 language from the Transportation Bill.

As Michael Fumento, a veteran writer on scientific subjects, puts it, "Even advocates of the .08 BAC limit admit that drivers below the .10 level rarely drive erratically; hence the only way to catch them is by putting up more police roadblocks and doing more random breath testing." Apart from harassing innocent drivers who have had a glass of wine or two over dinner, this has the pernicious side effect of diverting police away from patrolling the highways, where they might spot and pull over genuinely dangerous drunks, Fumento argues.

But MADD marches on, arguing that drunk drivers are responsible for 40 to 50 per cent of all highway fatalities. In this, MADD operates in collusion with the NHTSA, which misleadingly defines as "alcohol-related" *all* traffic fatalities where *any* trace level of alcohol—no matter how small—is discovered in the bloodstream of any person involved in the accident, *even if it's not the driver.*

The NHTSA is working hard in the campaign to lower BAC standards, even if it means playing fast and loose with the evidence. James Fell, the NHTSA's chief of research and evaluation at the time, testified in January 1998 before a committee of the Minnesota House that was considering legislation to lower Minnesota's threshold for drunk-driving arrests from .10 to .08 BAC. Fell claimed that the state of California had experienced a 12 per cent reduction in alcohol-related fatalities after it adopted the .08 BAC threshold.

But it turns out that that figure was a *prediction* made by a consultant in favor of the .08 limit. In fact, following the implementation of the .08 BAC threshold, California's alcohol-related deaths declined 6.1 per cent—slightly less than the country-wide decline of 6.3 per cent over that same period.

One definite effect of lowering the standard, as Dr. Ross points out, would be more arrests. For MADD, that would justify more lobbying, more contributions, more PR campaigns, more business for itself. "Like any successful firm," says Rick Berman, "MADD has recognized an iron rule: Revenue must exceed expenses. The tale of the tape is unmistakable." Indeed, MADD enjoyed a cash flow of $45.5 million in 1994. It has become one of the most powerful, well-funded, and omnipresent lobbying groups in the country.

For this success to continue, the battle against drunk driving can never appear to be won. And the need for new laws can never seem to be sated. Candy Lightner puts it mildly: "I worry that the movement I helped create has lost direction."

THE LIABILITY OF BUSINESSES THAT SERVE ALCOHOL TO DRUNK DRIVERS

Don Dzikowski

Dram shop laws allow parties who are injured by a drunk driver to obtain monetary damages from establishments that knowingly contributed to the driver's intoxication by serving him or her alcohol. This liability is also extended to survivors if the accident proves fatal. In the following selection, journalist Don Dzikowski describes the alternatives available to restaurant and tavern owners who want to avoid liability for damage that might be caused by their inebriated patrons. Although many authorities believe that liability insurance should be mandatory for businesses that serve alcohol, he notes that a significant number of businesses are unable to afford or refuse to obtain liability insurance. Businesses are also frustrated with the inconsistency in dram shop laws from state to state, Dzikowski writes. According to the author, another option is to educate business owners and their employees on ways to recognize signs of intoxication, modify drinking behavior, and slow the intoxication of customers, thus helping to reduce the likelihood that patrons will drive while drunk.

The restaurant and tavern industry has a way to go in curbing alcohol-related injuries and deaths.

Nationwide, the number of wrongful death lawsuits decided against alcohol establishments has quadrupled since 1988, according to the Insurance Information Institute.

In addition, the institute and Mothers Against Drunk Driving (MADD) point out that restaurants and bars play a substantial role in drunk-driving accidents. Alcohol was present in the blood of 41.3 percent of the people who died in auto accidents in 1995, according to the institute.

If drunk driving is not significantly reduced, the groups warn, two out of every five Americans will be involved in an alcohol-related accident at some point in their lives. . . .

Reprinted, by permission of Westfair Communications, Inc., from "Curbing Alcohol Abuse: Adequate Training Can Reduce a Bar Owner's Liability Exposure," by Don Dzikowski, *Fairfield County (Conn.) Business Journal*, August 4, 1997.

The Alternatives to Dram Shop Laws

But are restaurants and bars making the best effort possible to reduce alcohol-related incidents? Some members of the legal and restaurant communities question whether liquor liability—or dram shop—laws governing establishments in Connecticut, New York and elsewhere, as well as voluntary nationwide training programs for commercial servers of alcohol, go far enough.

Alfred Laub, a White Plains, New York, attorney specializing in dram shop litigation, questions whether the nature of the business makes change possible. Bar and restaurant owners must balance the economic incentive to pour as many drinks as possible with an ethical duty to protect patrons and their potential victims. "The two motives are not often compatible," Laub said.

Many local bars are geared towards a younger crowd, promoting "happy hours" and "half-price drink nights." A routine feature are voluptuous young females, who wear little clothing besides a belt of liquor bottles, and pass through the crowds offering shots or "shooters" in test tubes.

Fred Del Marva, a nationally recognized expert in liquor liability, barroom security and dram shop litigation, said broader education of alcohol servers would result in fewer drunks on the highways. For a nominal fee, bar and restaurant owners can participate in nationwide training programs such as TIPS (training of intervention procedures) and TAM (techniques of alcohol management) that are subsidized by the liquor industry. Extended courses teach owners how to become certified trainers so that they can instruct their own employees.

Participants learn how to recognize visible signs of intoxication, how food, weight and other factors can affect the rate of intoxication, and how to discretely modify a customer's drinking behavior.

ITT Hartford, Continental and other major insurance companies offer lower liquor liability insurance premiums for bar owners who complete TIPS or TAM training. CIGNA California, for example, gives a 10 to 25 percent discount to establishments that complete TIPS courses.

Since 1987, Del Marva has been retained in more than 175 cases (by both plaintiff and defense) in 25 states including Connecticut and New York. He testified in the Las Vegas "Tailhook" case and other high-profile cases. He is chief executive officer of Del Marva Corp. in Novato, California, which provides special events security and consulting for food and beverage investigations.

Del Marva said many owners participate in training to take advantage of lower insurance rates, but they are not passing on the knowledge to the bartenders and waiters who actually serve the customers. "It sounds good. (The owner) tells the courts 'I have TIPS.' But in depositions, you find the employees don't have any idea how to spot an intoxicated person."

A responsible alcohol server must be able to detect the warning signs and be willing to cut someone off, he said.

The industry also has failed to set standards on how to best design bars and adjoining parking lots to set up deterrents for alcohol-induced fights, Del Marva said.

MADD and other groups advocate training as a prerequisite to obtaining a license to serve alcohol, but only the state of Nevada has adopted such a measure, Del Marva said.

The Liability Insurance Question

About half of restaurants and taverns nationwide have no liquor liability insurance or dram shop coverage, industry insiders said. These establishments don't want to pay the extra costs required for the insurance, which in the metropolitan region can average between $5,000 to $10,000 a year for a small tavern and $200 to $2,000 a year for a neighborhood restaurant. Rates are based on the percentage of business involving alcohol.

Del Marva blamed industry lobbyists for defeating proposals to compel establishments to carry liquor liability coverage. In Connecticut, a measure that failed to pass the 1997 General Assembly session would have mandated liquor liability coverage for all businesses serving alcohol.

Simon Flynn, president of the Connecticut Restaurant Association in Glastonbury, said his group opposed the measure as an "economic burden on small business." A more equitable solution would be to educate bartenders, said Flynn, adding the association helps sponsor local TIPS and TAM courses. The group also participates in designated driver and MADD sponsored programs.

"We teach our members that there's no economic incentive to over-sell (alcoholic beverages)," Flynn said. "We tell them one fatal accident and they are in jeopardy. Their entire business can come crashing down."

In New York state, Scott Wexler, executive director of the Empire State Restaurant & Tavern Association in Albany, said his group supports legislation that would require owners to demonstrate knowledge of the liquor liability laws, as well as TIPS-style awareness training, as a prerequisite for receiving a state license to serve alcohol.

"We find there's a lot of misinformation out there," said Wexler. "We find businesses are getting hit with lawsuits because they don't know the laws."

Wexler said recent surveys of association members found some bar owners in the state believe they have a right to use a baseball bat to remove an intoxicated patron from their premises. "That's assault and battery," he said.

Owners should look for creative ways to sell food products to accompany drinks, he added. For example, sales of chicken wings can be profitable while providing a "fat and greasy" food to absorb the alcohol and slow intoxication.

Wexler said many of the group's 6,000 members frown on mandated liquor liability insurance because they believe the coverage makes them vulnerable to attorneys seeking monetary settlements from insurance companies on behalf of less-than-scrupulous clients. "There's a problem when you have the insurance. You become a target of lawsuits," he said.

The Dram Shop Laws

Insiders note that most states have adopted dram shop laws, which allow parties who have been injured—or their survivors in the event of a fatal incident—due to the intoxication of another individual to recover monetary damages against any person or establishment, including retail stores, taverns and restaurants, that knowingly cause such intoxication.

Courts and legislatures nationwide have discarded the "archaic notion" that a person is responsible for his own drunken behavior. It is now widely held that both the patron and the tavern owner who serves him share responsibility.

To establish a dram shop claim, attorneys must provide proof of their clients' intoxication at the time of the incident, proof of intoxication at the time of the service of alcohol, and proof of culpability of the alcohol server (i.e. that the bartender should have known the individual was drunk at the time of service).

Laws vary from state to state, and that has generated controversy in the industry.

In New York, there are no limits to the amount of money an injured party can receive, according to Laub. A claim must be filed within three years (or one year and 90 days for claims forwarded by municipal employees).

Laub won settlements of nearly $300,000 in dram shop cases against a Hilton Hotel franchise and a karaoke cafe located in New York state.

Dram shop laws are different in Connecticut, said Stewart M. Casper, a Stamford attorney and immediate past president of the Connecticut Trial Lawyers Association.

A Connecticut alcohol server cannot be found liable for more than $20,000 per injured person, or more than $50,000 for multiple injured parties per incident. Some states that have similar caps on damage awards allow aggrieved parties to seek higher compensation through common law negligence statutes as well, but not Connecticut.

The prevailing law in Connecticut has been that claims for injuries caused by alcohol intoxication cannot be made under statutes of common law negligence. (The only exception is if the individual who caused the injury was under the age of 21 and was served alcohol). An aggrieved party has 60 days from time of incident to file a claim, and one year to file a lawsuit.

Casper believes Connecticut's dram shop laws are too lenient on bar and restaurant owners. "It's a crime the limits are not higher. If they were, state bar owners would be a whole lot more careful not to serve a drunk."

Del Marva agreed that capping awards is a poor deterrent. "Too many bar owners share the mentality that it's not a big deal to risk losing $50,000," Del Marva said. "They think if they start serving responsibly they'll lose [drink sales] and lose $100,000 a year."

Caps are based on the outdated concept that the bartender should only be held responsible in a limited way for the actions of a person buying the drinks.

Casper doesn't like the 60-day limit for filing a claim in Connecticut, noting that police often take longer than that to pinpoint the establishment responsible for serving an intoxicated party who causes an accident. . . .

One problem the bar owners find with the dram shop laws is how their business can be targeted for liability, even when an intoxicated individual had 10 drinks at "the bar down the street" before ever setting foot into their establishments.

As bar owner Tom Brennan put it, even if the customer only has a beer in your place—if it's his last stop before causing an accident, "you still can get screwed."

Defending Drunk Drivers: Lawyers Who Advertise on the Internet

Bill Adler Jr.

In the following selection, Bill Adler Jr. describes the advertisements placed on the Internet by lawyers who claim they can guarantee a successful drunk driving defense. Adler argues that these lawyers are encouraging drunk driving by advertising that they can successfully defend people who were arrested for driving with very high blood alcohol levels or who have had their driver's license suspended or revoked. He also gives examples of advertisements that actually suggest how to avoid getting caught when drinking and driving. Rather than promote ways for drivers to avoid responsibility, Adler concludes, these lawyers should work with society to prevent drunk driving. Adler is an author and literary agent.

Internet pornography. Hate groups. Instructions for building bombs. Fraudulent money-making schemes. These are some of the abuses of the Internet. But one of the most outrageous—even frightening— abuses of the medium is by lawyers who advertise their ability to get drunk drivers off the hook.

I'm not talking about attorneys defending people merely accused of drunk driving, but lawyers who brag about their ability to win not-guilty verdicts for even the most assuredly guilty drivers with high blood alcohol levels. Now, I'm sure some of you are thinking: "Everybody has a right to a fair trial, and there are probably a lot of people accused of driving under the influence (DUI) who aren't really guilty. So what's the harm of lawyers defending people accused of drunk driving?" Fundamentally, there's nothing wrong with it. It's vital that everyone have the best legal representation possible. But this new breed of online advertisement implies—and in many cases states outright—that it doesn't matter if you drive drunk, because these legal eagles can bail you out. In short, they are promoting the notion that it's okay to drive as drunk as you want.

Reprinted, by permission of *The Washington Monthly*, from "A Deadly Mix: Drinking, Driving, and Lawyers on the Information Superhighway," by Bill Adler Jr., *The Washington Monthly*, July/August 1998. Copyright by The Washington Monthly Company, 1611 Connecticut Ave. NW, Washington, DC 20009.

Advertising the Defense of Drunk Driving

Think I'm exaggerating? I'll let the lawyers' words speak for themselves. Here are excerpts from actual web sites. One lawyer from San Diego boasts, "You need an aggressive attorney to keep you out of jail and who has experience in hundreds of DUI & DMV [Department of Motor Vehicles] matters like yours!" His site then lists the blood alcohol content (BAC) of the clients for whom he's had legal victories:

Client	BAC%	Type of Test
Backesto	.15–.16	Blood+Breath/Under 21/Accident
Bonas	.15	Breath
Briggs	.16	Breath
Callaway	.09	Blood
Caster	.17	Blood
Costa	.13	Breath

To put these numbers in context, if your blood alcohol level is above .10, you are legally drunk in all states. In some states the limit is .08. But don't worry, because this lawyer insists he can successfully defend you even if your blood alcohol level is .17.

Another lawyer publishes an online newsletter for people arrested for drunk driving. Here's his pitch:

You have just been arrested and charged with a crime. Since one of the charges is DUI, you probably spent a few hours in jail before they released you with a ticket ordering you to appear in court, or you may have posted bail. . . . Don't be cheated by anyone in the process, especially yourself. Legal representation will prepare you for success in the court and DMV processes.

Yet another lawyer, billing himself as a "Top Gun DUI Defense Attorney," brags:

We have over 40 years combined experience successfully representing doctors, lawyers, professional athletes, business people, and others accused of DUI. Some of our recent successes include our client who was arrested for DUI and blew .28. Another client was arrested for his 3rd DUI and blew a .16. Another client was arrested for DUI after an accident and blew a .16. Another client was arrested for DUI after an accident with injuries and measured a .11 blood. Another client was arrested for his 2nd DUI and blew a .10. Still another client was arrested for her 2nd DUI and blew a .12. Five of these six clients had their license suspension/revocation set aside by the DMV. The bottom line is that we successfully represent many of our clients charged with DUI!

When should you challenge a DUI arrest? According to a Colorado lawyer, when "you don't think it's fair." (When does a defendant ever think an arrest is "fair"?) This lawyer goes on to say, "I know you're fearful about what could happen to you, but I'd like you to know that there are at least 20 different challenges that can be made to the charges you are facing. . . . My practice is based on the belief that you were arrested when you shouldn't have been."

Still another attorney crows:

> Where jury trials are available, success rates for acquittal are surprisingly good. . . . The formula for success is to investigate exhaustively; conduct pretrial discovery and motion practice aggressively; use evidentiary maneuvers and procedural devices skillfully; and present a well-conceived, thoroughly choreographed trial with expert witnesses, character witnesses, and other tried-and-true tactics for successful defense of criminal cases.

On one particularly "helpful" site, two lawyers hawk their book, *101 Ways to Avoid a Drunk Driving Conviction,* promising to reveal "the secrets that prosecutors, judges, and other special interest groups don't want you to know." These lawyers give advice on how to drive while intoxicated and reduce your chances of ever getting caught: "'Blend in' with traffic because studies have shown that it is significantly more difficult for police to detect an impaired driver than when your car is isolated on the highway." In their book you also learn that:

> Requiring strict proof of the testing officer's certification can often lead to a dismissal or a favorable "plea bargain" where some flaw or defect in the proof of current certification is called into question. By asking the officer whether you can make telephone calls to an attorney or family member prior to submitting the official BAC tests, you may be taking advantage of legally permissible delays that will make your BAC tests more favorable.

Indeed, tips on how to avoid being arrested for drunk driving are part of many lawyers' web sites, all in the name of good advertising. One Georgia attorney writes, "Don't tempt fate. Before leaving a bar parking lot, check to see if there are any cops in the area. If so, wait until the cops follow another person from the lot, and then leave."

What about suggesting that drivers simply abstain from driving after drinking? No. Instead the advice focuses on not getting caught. There's even a "Drunk Driving Defense Network" and "National College for Drunk Driving Defense" on the Internet. The National College site, designed for lawyers, also teaches habitual drunk drivers how to avoid being stopped for DUI. Some lawyers place the blame for drunk driving on the government. One attorney writes, "The crime of drunk driving occurs only when the person's blood-alcohol level has exceeded the arbitrary numerical standard set by the state"

It's not surprising that lawyers aggressively pursue drunk driving clients. Each year, nearly 2 million drivers are charged with driving under the influence, making drunk driving the single most common criminal offense in the country. That's a lot of potential business. "Call now for a free consultation," urges one Florida lawyer.

More than just "smart business," however, this kind of advertising makes it easier for drivers to believe, "Well, if I'm caught driving drunk, a good lawyer can get me off." Bottom line: These lawyers are encouraging people to drive drunk.

There's something terribly wrong here. Each year more than 17,000 people are killed by drunk drivers, and hundreds of thousands more are injured. Drunk drivers cause 41 percent of all fatal crashes. Ethically, there's no difference between lawyers soliciting to get drunk drivers off the hook and advertising along the lines of: "Accused of Murder? Call John Q. Smith, attorney. We have a 75 percent acquittal rate!" Drunk driving is something society should be working together to stop. Lawyers shouldn't be promoting ways to get offenders off the hook just to make an easy buck.

ORGANIZATIONS TO CONTACT

The editors have compiled the following list of organizations concerned with the issues presented in this book. Descriptions are derived from materials provided by the organizations. All have publications or information available for interested readers. The list was compiled on the date of publication of the present volume; names, addresses, phone and fax numbers, and e-mail/Internet addresses may change. Be aware that many organizations take several weeks or longer to respond to inquiries, so allow as much time as possible.

Against Drunk Driving (ADD)
PO Box 397, Station A, Brampton, ON L6V 2L3 Canada
(905) 793-4233 • fax: (905) 793-7035
e-mail: add@netcom.ca • website: www.add.ca

Founded in 1983, ADD is a grassroots organization that strives to reduce death and injury caused by impaired drivers through educating the public about the dangers of drunk driving. The organization's Victims Self-Help program provides counseling for people who have lost loved ones in drunk driving accidents. ADD also holds presentations for alcohol-impaired drivers in correctional facilities as part of a six-week rehabilitation program called GUARD (Greater Understanding on Alcohol Related Driving). ADD's group for young adults, Teen-ADD, holds conferences, workshops, and presentations to raise awareness about the problem of teen drunk driving. ADD publishes the quarterly newsletter *ADDvisor*, which is also available on its website.

Boaters Against Drunk Driving (BADD)
141-B Landmark St., Deltona, FL 32725-8027
(407) 574-7153
e-mail: SafeBoating@badd.org • website: www.badd.org

BADD is dedicated to promoting safe, sober, and responsible boating throughout the United States and Canada. Through its Judicial Watch, the organization monitors cases of individuals charged with boating under the influence of alcohol (BUI); BADD publishes the progress of these cases to demonstrate to the boating community and the general public that state boating officials, legislators, prosecutors, and courts all consider BUI a very serious crime. As a memorial to the victims of BUI tragedies, BADD has implemented a project called Lighthouse of Law. BADD's website also includes statistics, charts, and articles concerning the dangers of boating under the influence of alcohol.

Center for Substance Abuse Prevention (CSAP)
National Clearinghouse for Alcohol and Drug Information (NCADI)
PO Box 2345, Rockville, MD 20847-2345
(800) 729-6686 • fax: (301) 468-6433
e-mail: info@health.org • website: www.health.org

The CSAP leads U.S. government efforts to prevent alcoholism and other substance abuse problems among Americans. Through the NCADI, the center provides the public with a wide variety of information concerning alcohol abuse, including the problem of drunk driving. Its publications include the bimonthly *Prevention Pipeline*, the report "Impaired Driving Among Youth: Trends and Tools for Prevention," brochures, pamphlets, videotapes, and posters. Publications in Spanish are also available.

Century Council
1310 G St. NW, Suite 600, Washington, DC 20005
(202) 637-0077 • fax: (202) 637-0079
e-mail: jonesb@centurycouncil.org • website: www.centurycouncil.org

Funded by America's leading distillers, the Century Council is a not-for-profit, national organization committed to fighting underage drinking and reducing alcohol-related crashes. The council promotes legislative efforts to pass tough drunk driving laws and works with the alcohol industry to help servers and sellers prevent drunk driving. Its interactive CD-ROM, *Alcohol 101*, provides "virtual" scenarios to help students make sensible, fact-based decisions about drinking.

Distilled Spirits Council of the United States (DISCUS)
1250 Eye St. NW, Suite 400, Washington, DC 20005
(202) 628-3544
website: www.discus.health.org

The Distilled Spirits Council of the United States is the national trade association representing producers and marketers of distilled spirits in the United States. It seeks to ensure the responsible use of distilled spirits by adult consumers and to curb alcohol abuse and underage drinking. DISCUS publishes fact sheets, the periodic newsletter *News Release*, and several pamphlets, including *The Drunk Driving Prevention Act*.

Entertainment Industries Council (EIC)
1760 Reston Pkwy., Suite 415, Reston, VA 20190-3330
(703) 481-1414 • fax: (703) 481-1418
e-mail: eic@eiconline.org • website: www.eiconline.org

The EIC works to educate the entertainment industry and audiences about major public health and social issues. Its members strive to effect social change by providing educational materials, research, and training to the entertainment industry. The EIC publishes several fact sheets concerning alcohol abuse and alcohol-impaired driving.

Mothers Against Drunk Driving (MADD)
PO Box 541688, Dallas, TX 75354-1688
(214) 744-6233 • fax: (214) 869-2209
e-mail: info@madd.org • website: www.madd.org

A nationwide grassroots organization, MADD provides support services to victims of drunk driving and attempts to influence policy makers by lobbying for changes in legislation on local, state, and national levels. MADD's public education efforts include its "Rating the States" report, which draws attention to the status of state and federal efforts against drunk driving. MADD publishes the semiannual *Driven* magazine and numerous pamphlets and brochures, including *Someone You Know Drinks and Drives, Financial Recovery After a Drunk Driving Crash*, and *Drunk Driving: An Unacknowledged Form of Child Endangerment*.

National Commission Against Drunk Driving (NCADD)
1900 L St. NW, Suite 705, Washington, DC 20036
(202) 452-6004 • fax: (202) 223-7012
e-mail: ncadd@trafficsafety.org • website: www.ncadd.com

NCADD comprises public and private sector leaders who are dedicated to minimizing the human and economic losses resulting from motor vehicle crashes by making impaired driving a socially unacceptable act. Working with private sector groups and federal, state, and local officials, NCADD develops strategies to target the three most intractable groups of drunk drivers: underage drinkers, young adults, and chronic drunk drivers. The commission's publications include research abstracts, traffic safety facts, the reports "The Dummy's Guide to Youth Alcohol Programs" and "Chronic Drunk Drivers: Resources Available to Keep Them off the Road," and a guide for parent/teen discussion, "Yes, You May Use the Car, but FIRST . . .".

National Highway Traffic Safety Administration (NHTSA)
Impaired Driving Division
400 Seventh St. SW, Washington, DC 20590
(202) 366-2683 ext. 2728
website: www.nhtsa.dot.gov/people/injury/alcohol

The NHTSA allocates funds for states to demonstrate the effectiveness of visible enforcement initiatives against drunk driving. The mission of its Impaired Driving Division is to save lives, prevent injuries, and reduce traffic-related health care and economic costs resulting from impaired driving. The organization's publications concerning impaired driving include the pamphlet *Get the Keys* and the manual *Strategies for Success: Combating Juvenile DUI*, which provides tools to help develop a comprehensive criminal justice system response to underage drunk driving.

Students Against Destructive Decisions (SADD)
PO Box 800, Marlboro, MA 01752
(508) 481-3568 • fax: (508) 481-5759
website: www.saddonline.com

Formerly called Students Against Drunk Driving, SADD is a school-based organization dedicated to addressing the issues of underage drinking, impaired driving, drug use, and other destructive decisions that harm young people. SADD seeks to provide students with prevention and intervention tools that build the confidence needed to make healthy choices and behavioral changes. These tools include "never again" campaigns in honor of students killed in drunk driving accidents, candlelight vigils, impact scenarios, and student surveys on teens' attitudes and concerns about drinking and driving. SADD also holds conferences and publishes a triannual newsletter.

BIBLIOGRAPHY

Books

Nathan Aaseng — *Teens and Drunk Driving.* San Diego, CA: Lucent Books, 2000.

Charles K. Atkin, William DeJong, and Lawrence Wallack — *The Influence of Responsible Drinking TV Spots and Automobile Commercials on Young Drivers.* Washington, DC: AAA Foundation for Traffic Safety, 1992.

Deborah Chrisfield — *Drinking and Driving.* Mankato, MN: Crestwood House, 1995.

Robyn L. Cohen — *Drunk Driving.* Washington, DC: U.S. Department of Justice, 1992.

Denis Foley, ed. — *Stop DWI: Successful Community Responses to Drunk Driving.* Lexington, MA: Lexington Books, 1986.

Sandy Golden — *How to Save Lives and Reduce Injuries: A Citizen Activist Guide to Effectively Fight Drunk Driving.* Washington, DC: U.S. Department of Transportation, 1983.

Janet Grosshandler-Smith — *Working Together Against Drinking and Driving.* New York: Rosen, 1996.

Janet Grosshandler-Smith and Ruth C. Rosen — *Coping with Drinking and Driving.* New York: Rosen, 1997.

James B. Jacobs — *Drunk Driving: An American Dilemma.* Chicago: University of Chicago Press, 1989.

Jean McBee Knox — *Drinking, Driving, and Drugs.* New York: Chelsea House, 1998.

Richard A. Leiter, ed. — *National Survey of State Laws.* Detroit: Gale Research, 1997.

Roy Light — *Criminalizing the Drink-Driver.* Brookfield, VT: Ashgate, 1994.

Gerald D. Robin — *Waging the Battle Against Drunk Driving.* Westport, CT: Greenwood, 1991.

H. Lawrence Ross — *Confronting Drunk Driving: Social Policy for Saving Lives.* New Haven: Yale University Press, 1992.

Frank A. Sloan, ed. — *Drinkers, Drivers, and Bartenders: Balancing Private Choices and Public Accountability.* Chicago: University of Chicago Press, 2000.

R. Jean Wilson and Robert E. Mann, eds. — *Drinking and Driving: Advances in Research and Prevention.* New York: Guildford, 1998.

Periodicals

Patrick Bedard — "The Deadly Drivers Are Deadly Drunk," *Car & Driver,* September 1998.

Patrick Bedard   "One Drink over the Line," *Car & Driver*, September
                          1998.

Richard Berman   "NHTSA Must Examine the Whole Truth to Be
                          Effective," *Nation's Restaurant News*, June 30, 1997.
                          Available from 425 Park Ave., New York, NY 10022.

Paula Brook   "The Ones Who Get Away: Drunks at the Wheel,"
                          Chatelaine, December 1996. Available from 777 Bay
                          St., 8th Floor, Toronto, ON M5W1A7 Canada.

William J. Clinton   "Remarks on Signing a Memorandum on Standards to
                          Prevent Drinking and Driving," *Weekly Compilation of
                          Presidential Documents*, March 9, 1998. Available from
                          the U.S. Government Printing Office, Superintendent
                          of Documents, PO Box 371954, Pittsburgh, PA 15250-
                          7954.

Kevin E. Courtright   "The Cost Effectiveness of Using House Arrest with
et al.   Electronic Monitoring for Drunk Drivers," *Federal
                          Probation*, September 1997.

Thomas Fields-Meyer   "Road Warrior," *People*, May 4, 1998.
and Grace Lim

Nora Fitzgerald   "Under the Influence," *Adweek-Western Edition*, June
                          15, 1998. Available from 1515 Broadway, New York,
                          NY 10036-8986.

Peter Grier   "Drunk Driving Draws Global Wrath," *Christian
                          Science Monitor*, September 3, 1997.

Allison Hatfield   "Canada's No-Criminals Rule," *Overdrive*, February
                          1997. Available from 3200 Rice Mine Rd. NE,
                          Tuscaloosa, AL 35406.

Ralph Hingson and   "Lowering State Legal Blood Alcohol Limits to 0.08%:
Timothy Heeren   The Effect on Fatal Motor Vehicle Crashes," *American
                          Journal of Public Health*, September 1996.

Jeff Kass   "Why the West Has Resisted Drunken-Driving Crack-
                          down," *Christian Science Monitor*, November 15, 1999.

Joey Kennedy   "Drunk Driving Makes a Comeback," *Redbook*, May
                          1997.

Li Way Lee   "The Socioeconomics of Drunk Driving," *Journal of
                          Socio-Economics*, 1997. Available from 100 Prospect St.,
                          PO Box 811, Stamford, CT 06904-0811.

Cathy Mikkel   "You Can Run, but You Can't Hide," *Motor Trend*,
                          August 1998.

Alan K. Ota   "Drunken-Driving Plan Stirs Controversy,"
                          Congressional Quarterly Weekly Report, March 7, 1998.
                          Available from 1414 22nd St. NW, Washington, DC
                          20037.

Peter J. Roeper and   "Underage Drivers Are Separating Drinking from
Robert B. Voas   Driving," *American Journal of Public Health*, May 1999.

Anne Russell and   "MADD Rates the States: A Media Advocacy Event to
Robert B. Voas   Advance the Agenda Against Alcohol-Impaired

Driving," *Public Health Reports*, May/June 1995.
Available from the U.S. Government Printing Office,
Superintendent of Documents, PO Box 371954,
Pittsburgh, PA 15250-7954.

Ruth Russell   "The Wounds That Can't Be Stitched Up," *Newsweek*,
December 20, 1999.

Herb Simpson   "Drunk, Dangerous, and Deadly," *Vital Speeches of the
Day*, November 1, 1999.

Jason K. Wells   "Drinking Drivers Missed at Sobriety Checkpoints,"
Journal of Studies on Alcohol, September 1997.

INDEX